Thank Goodness For Cake

A selection of John Pudney's books

THE NET
THE THOMAS COOK STORY
A RING FOR LUCK
THE SMALLEST ROOM
TRESPASS IN THE SUN
THE TRAMPOLINE
HOME AND AWAY
THE AIR
CROSSING LONDON'S RIVER
BRUNEL AND HIS WORLD
SELECTED POEMS
LONDON'S DOCKS
LEWIS CARROLL AND HIS WORLD
FOR JOHNNY—POEMS OF WORLD WAR II
LIVING IN A ONE-SIDED HOUSE
A LONG TIME GROWING UP

JOHN PUDNEY

THANK GOODNESS FOR CAKE

London
MICHAEL JOSEPH

First published in Great Britain by Michael Joseph Limited
52 Bedford Square, London WC1B 3EF
1978

© Monica Forbes Pudney 1978

All Rights Reserved. No part of this publication
may be reproduced, stored in a retrieval system,
or transmitted in any form or by any means,
electronic, mechanical, photocopying, recording
or otherwise, without the prior permission of the
Copyright owner

ISBN 0 7181 1732 8

Filmset in Great Britain by
Northumberland Press, Gateshead
Printed and bound by Redwood Burn,
Trowbridge and Esher

Contents

THANK GOODNESS FOR CAKE 7

THE FIRST AND LAST OF THE BOOZE 13

SI DIEU N'EXISTAIT PAS, IL FAUDRAIT L'INVENTER 22

THE ONLY CHILD 30

NAMES 39

PLACES 56

THE SQUARE PEG 72

LOVING 80

VERSATILITY TIME 93

THE FIFTIES 108

GOING DOWN 121

COMING UP 134

NIL BY MOUTH 147

Thank Goodness For Cake

When I was fifty, I published what I called an 'autobiographical gambit' called *Home and Away*. It offered a cautious, may be well-mannered, urbane account of the accepted and the acceptable. No offence, no compelling interest. I had published my *Collected Poems* a year or so before. It seems to me now that I was getting up a neat literary funeral for myself, as the end of middle-age approached.

"If only you would take that literary smile off your face," I now find myself murmuring to that autobiographer, wrapped in genial diffidence two decades ago. That blameless book does not mention Cake, a persistent force in my life. Nor does it offer any hint that the writer, smiling away, was well into the booze and would be flat on his back as an acknowledged alcoholic before the volume had time to collect dust on the bookshelf.

Let me fill in first with Cake. It is the reality. Drink is the illusion. Drink blurs; Cake substantiates. Throughout my life I must have said to myself, 'Thank goodness for cake.' Only recently have I caught myself saying it aloud. An illness which took me up to the frontiers of death, cleared my head of many scruples, and of several deceptions dressed up as diversions. The sense of guilt I harboured about Cake broke loose. It was an acknowledgement of immaturity. It was belated, yet so potent that it helped to sustain my will to live—already fortified by the presence and prayers of loved ones. Cake offers security and serenity to that part of my nature which has stayed innocent, wondering, hopeful, puzzled—what is loosely described as immature. That word has been flung at me over the years, of course, as my shortcomings have revealed themselves, usually to those nearest and dearest. I have denied or retreated from the charge beneath a cloud of guilt, the cloud that hid Cake.

Some hint of my awareness does not react to growth or to so-called progress, to ambition, to the age patterns and conventions. This immaturity with its Cake symbol is potent yet not portentous. It is light-hearted almost to the point of frivolity. It is diffident, yet can be cruel. It can put my adult manhood in a corner wearing a dunce's cap. (That period word *dunce* has no place in my adult vocabulary.) Its laughter can resemble a jeer. Its most constant quality is that of wonderment. And it now seems absurd that guilt at 'not growing up' should have hidden that sense of wonderment. When experience, 'being your age', takes the edge off the scene and creates conventional responses, this sense of wonderment is turned on, secretly, dazzlingly, critically putting an edge on scene and response. It lingers only just long enough to affect decisions. It makes no protest at being ignored. It does not respond to beck and call. It simply reveals itself as a part of my nature. Cake is its manifestation. Cake is the reassurance that life is worth living. It is a moment of serenity, of wonder, of innocence.

Do I need such reassurance now, in old age, as I certainly needed them in youth and middle age? I need them as much for I am no better or worse. Floating on my back on the Thames near Runnymede, after learning to swim, I used to contemplate manhood, swimming being one up on a whole adult family of non-swimmers. What would it be like to be twenty-five like the dashing Maths master, Mr Nightingale with his own two-seater Citroën? How different would I feel at forty-five, the age of my Father, whose life was a routine of uneventful idleness? Would I be settled down in some kindly harmless uneventfulness? Or supposing one came to be sixty like George V up there on the ramparts of Windsor Castle? The old people were always on about the past. They were bloated, or shrivelled. Would I turn into something so totally different?

In my last swim and float on my back, I remembered all this. I was in the pool of Mena House Hotel and, as I idled in the water, I contemplated the Great Pyramid of Cheops just across the road. What a setting for a last swim, not that I knew it was the last, that on return to England I was to have a tracheotomy—which rules out immersion, even in the bath-tub at home. The grandiose, and totally unlikely setting sharpened the quest for identity. Was this really me who had first floated at Runnymede? Me, a man in his late sixties? Why did I not feel different, stronger, wiser? The surroundings were exotic to be sure (we were making a BBC film about Thomas Cook, the excursionist). But the body and the mind indolently pointing at the Great Pyramid had not changed significantly since they wore a boy's skin at Runnymede. I was so overawed by the ordinariness of myself, that I began a nice banal poem on a pool-side menu-card:

> Cheops, Cheops, are you all right
> To be so nearly immortal but not quite...

Among the amenities of Mena House was the offer of Cake.

I should explain perhaps that my day to day attitude toward Cake is not obsessive. I do not seek it out. I go for long periods without a sight of it. I do not even rate myself a connoisseur of Cake—certainly not a Cake-bore, carrying on the way people do about wine. It should be what is known as fruit cake, cut in slabs or slices. Gâteaux, and all the arts of the pastry cook are out symbolically, even though they may be compulsive eating. None of the dainties, such as rock cakes, éclairs, doughnuts, welcome as they come, possess the Cake status.

Though the eating of it is desirable, it is not essential. Seeing it there, on offer, is the magic. The eating of it, particularly if it is homemade and rich, is a bonus. It can also be a hardship when it comes in cellophane packs at an airport.

The symbolism of Cake is, I suppose, steadfastly tied to childhood. I was too wary to discuss it with the two psychiatrists who treated me for alcoholism, but I am sure they would have had me regressing to my beginnings as an only child. That oneness affected attitudes, habits, sexuality and, indeed, love itself. That oneness looked anxiously for security but it was not in itself the origin of Cake.

I was born at Langley, Bucks, in 1909, in a gentrified farmhouse; it had its own cherry orchards and a few meadows; no electricity, gas or telephone. My father had retired from farming, while still on the right side of forty, and nobody could ever explain this. My mother died before my teenage curiosity could question her. I doubt if ever she really knew. After winning silver trophies, which I still possess, for such credits as 'the best barley' farming in the Runnymede area, he threw up regular work to live on a small private income at Langley. The extraordinary structure of idleness and non-eventfulness affected me more and more as I grew up within it, an only child. My mother, older than my father, big-boned, red-headed, and brought up mainly in Australia, was a trained nurse. A gregarious creature, she somehow conformed to this pattern. Her protests were non-accusative, and only just perceptible to me as I became old enough to receive them. The idea of this structure was that it should be secure and safe, mainly by nullifying action. There was no travel, except for occasional trips to members of the family at Canterbury and in Somerset. Visits to London were so rare that I was sick from excitement every time I went. Though Langley was already well settled, with commuters by the GWR to Paddington, the pretence of a three-rung rural society lingered for us. There were the gentry, such as Sir Robert Harvey in a melancholy decline in Langley Park. There were the working class and trades people who still called for orders. Between, was the precarious middle class of farmers, would-be farmers, gent-farmers and nurserymen. They, like my father, habitually wore breeches, even when the horses began to disappear. To the new people, the commuters, for all their wealth, tennis courts and motor-cars were regarded as inhabitants of another dimension.

So our social range consisted of a handful of families living out an Edwardian style, one or two domestics and a couple of horses in the stables. When I was five, the world began crashing. My mother nursed in a neighbouring mansion taken over as a hospital. My father suffered the martyrdom of war work in a factory a few stations up the line, and was referred to as my 'poor father'. When I asked if it wasn't better than being sent off to be killed, I was told not to be pert. I talked to myself and went about with imaginary companions—several people mentioned this later in my life. My first contact with boys of my own age, except for illicit contact with village boys, was when I went as a weekly boarder to a school in Slough. By the middle of the war there was no transport for daily school, so my first separation from home took place—bed-wetting, sleep-walking and loud nightmares contributed to the nocturnal show I put on.

In this childhood environment of hidden stress, inertia and

shifting values, there was surely little to generate a sense of security and create a life-long comfort in Cake. No, I think it goes deeper than childhood environment. As I was born in original sin, so I was also equipped with innocence, the unquenchable sense of wonderment. Which, perhaps too frivolously for some tastes, is symbolised in Cake.

The First and Last of the Booze

Nobody has proved that alcoholism is hereditary. Though there may be talk of its 'running in the family—look at Uncle George' the men and women who become alcoholics seem to come as much from teetotal or repressive environments, as from families in which drink is accessible as a matter of course. Some, seeking easy justification, blame their flight upon a single calamity such as breakdown of marriage, unrequited love, career failure or an occupational hazard. This is an over-simplification. The causes are varied and subtle, though of course they may include one or more of the stereotyped calamities. They are unique to the individual. Not least of them is a liking for the stuff, a factor sometimes overlooked in the search for deeper issues. A superficial survey of my own life, made by the psychiatrist, suggested at least a dozen causes contributing to my illness—with a full-blooded admission at the outset that I had loved the stuff.

One common denominator found in all fellow alcoholics is isolation. This is imposed by society, friends, work-mates, relatives and family. The malady is shushed-up, ignored, tolerated, hedged and fenced about by pride, love, hostility, shame. It is also self-imposed, the individual shrinking back more and more into such inner resources as survive. It becomes a secretive, furtive, double life; pulling down blinds, dodging people and events. The loner in company, in solitude the fugitive; that is the path of the alcoholic. It is miles away from the music-hall drunks, from the flamboyant genial jokery of over-drink. The sick person is not necessarily the one lying flat in the gutter. The very sick person goes to infinite pains to conceal the malady, even when in the private battlefield quite out of control. Alcoholics, in their isolation, are adept at cunning ploys and subterfuge. "But you carry your liquor so well. Such a wonderful head. You just can't be a ..." People (characteristically shying off the actual word), would say this to me when I became an acknowledged, and public alcoholic, on the social throes of recovery. There was some truth in this; the sad truth that while I was never recklessly drunk, I was never sober. The intake had been craftily and disastrously spread out over every twenty-four hours—with such organised items as the brandy miniature in the pyjama pocket for shaving time.

My progress in over-drink was unexceptional. I was a robust and hearty drinker, then a steady drinker, then a heavy drinker. The shift from that into alcoholism comes when the body takes over, the metabolism demanding a constant supply whatever the mind or the conscience may say. The image of drink is conviviality, that of over-drink is this desolate isolation; the realisation that there is no security at all in the homely beer, the noble wine, the rare brandy, any more than there is in the hidden nip taken to quell the shakes.

I cannot deny the pleasures of the forty drinking years. Wine first caressed my senses in Charlemagne's vineyards at Rüdesheim. I came to terms with the diversities of vodka in Warsaw and with those of schnapps in Stockholm. I learnt the meaning of a dry Martini in Manhattan. I was an ardent beer-from-the-wood fancier, with an eye for rewarding pubs in the British Isles. I developed a reasonable nose for wine. Five years after I had given up drinking, I was challenged by the late Raymond Postgate to place three reds in their order of quality, by nose alone, and I passed the test. I salute the pleasures and would not have been denied them. What disturbs me now, in hindsight, are the many elements other than pleasure which accompany drink. Even if I had not fallen a victim to over-drink—and many heavy drinkers never become alcoholics—the mysteries and habits of drinking which influenced my life from time to time were never to my advantage physically, philosophically or morally. Subtract the pleasure, and one is left with a potent array of forces, the more obvious being ritualism, social pressure, virility culture and conformity. Addiction may be the end product, to be alleviated only by abstinence. It is recognised as the rock bottom, the ultimate calamity, but is responsive to treatment. The damage is revealed and studied and even partially remedied. But, insufficiently revealed and charted are the obligations to drink, which masquerade as pleasure or usurp it altogether. Whatever the colour of the tune, the theme is always the quest for security; that illusion of security, so portentous, so insubstantial compared with an unbidden glimpse of cake.

For many of us, awareness of drink starts less with the pleasures of taste and smell, than with a desire to be grown up. To beg a little or steal some is an escape from childhood into the imagined security of adult life. Here is a short cut from boyhood to manhood. Some unpleasant sidekicks. Uplift possible, but not guaranteed.

The image which grows out of this is that of virility—and it is a stayer. "Look at the way he sinks those pints! He's a real man." Capacity for liquor is equated with masculinity. Hence a further step—to sexuality. For several decades, brewers' advertising has emphasised the real manliness of beer, and the appeal somewhat mystifyingly extends to women. Wine and spirit purveyors delight to take a more sophisticated line in equating the product with boudoir forays and sexual adventures. To the young man, the message is persistent; not just through the media, but at every turn in social and working life. The real man can take it. To be a real man, he must take it. He must take a lot and hold it to be a hero. Above all, to be accepted as one of the tribe, it is essential to drink and stand your round. There's something funny about a bloke who doesn't.

These pressures work at all social levels. The virility cult is several generations deep. Only in the seventies have I noticed a generation which does not seem to be so hooked on the virility myth. A so-called permissive generation shows signs of indifference to the obligations of drink, while not being averse to its pleasures.

For me, before I was twenty, the obligations were accepted without question. The virility image held sway. A manly pipe jutted from my beardless mouth. A wallop of beer, preferably in a tankard, stood at my elbow. In those early years, I was a wet smoker and the pipe made me feel sick. The beer in the tankard was sometimes palatable, sometimes nauseating. The smoke and the drink were not just enjoyable for what they were, but for what they appeared to be. The unappetising reality that a tobacco-curried, drink-sodden bed companion might not prove all that virile, was not a subject for sympathetic discussion like a hangover, but a misgiving to be kept secret.

My first and my last drinks were both affairs of obligation. Not counting the sips of sherry or port bestowed by grown-ups in childhood, and a few cautious tipples on festive family occasions, my first drink, ordered and bought by myself, was draught beer in a tankard at Lyons Corner House, Coventry Street. The taste was new; a little agreeable, a little alarming. But this was manhood. I had started work on my seventeenth birthday, 19 January 1926, the year of the General Strike, and the trip to the Corner House at lunchtime was a celebration of my first pay day. It was incredibly glamorous. A ladies' band played, the waitresses were dashing, the individual steak-and-kidney pudding was almost within one's means. My companion—we dutched of course—was an older man, almost into his twenties. "How do you find the beer here?" he enquired, sucking froth from his incipient moustache.

"Not too bad at all," I assured him, wondering how I should ever get to the bottom of the tankard.

"Surprising what Joe Lyons can put up." My companion spoke as a man of the world. "I hope it don't make you sleepy this afternoon."

The more pressing problem was how to live till the afternoon, and to contain this outrageous quantity of brown liquid, this man's drink bought with my own money.

My companion grinned and said, "We mustn't be late back. Bottoms up, old chap."

That myth was finally disposed of with my last tipple, forty years later almost to the day, at breakfast time with no band playing. Following a double whisky, which had gone down somewhat reluctantly on a lagoon of Chateau Neuf, I was offered a measure of Remy Martin by the smiling doctor. "Your old favourite once again." I winced as I took it, praying that it might be the last obligatory drink and that there should not be that genial command: "Just one more..."

This was indeed the substance without the symbolism, the climax of an aversion treatment. The good healthy drink in my mouth did not symbolise manhood or security, only a body's frailty.

"Drink it right down now. Bottoms up." The doctor beamed.

The nurse brought the sick bowl within range. "There now, perhaps we'll have it all up?"

My whole nature disintegrated as the empty glass slid through my fingers and my body quaked.

Some hours later, the doctor, dropping the geniality, said, "With a little help, you should be able to live without it." That means not feeling deprived or unmanned, not indulging in self-pity or smug saintliness, discovering that life without liquor is normal.

Such was the beginning and the end of forty years of conviviality. The end was not achieved without what the doctor called 'a little help'. The isolation, the potency of the physical need, the disarray of values cannot be broken and sudued by the alcoholic without support. There may be rare cases where a loner has done it, but I have never found one. The loner, after all, has to be taken out of self-imposed isolation. This can only be done with love, the friendship, and the concern of others. That is by family, friends, priest, psychiatrist, social worker or doctor.

Recovery is not just an event, but a continuing process. It is certainly not cure, full stop. It begins as a new life euphorically and perilously opening out. A sense of physical well-being, or need to make up for lost time. Over-confidence and feverish amend-making go to form a light-headed mixture common to recovered alcoholics. It can wreck relationships which have survived the hazards of over-drink. For instance, the man who for years could not entertain in his own home, and had to telephone from his office every day to check his wife's affair with the bottle, suddenly finds himself released from his custodian duties. The suddenness of the liberation is too much for both of them. He cannot break himself of custodial concern—those timely telephone calls. She takes each one as a sign of not being trusted. Conversely, for the woman, whose husband has recovered, there can be quite a strong and unacknowledged sense of anti-climax, like the loss of a dependant child. It had become second nature for my wife to demand a timed itinerary every time I went off for the day. How unthinkingly I resented this.

My own treatment at the hands of Dr Lincoln Williams and Dr Rodney Long left me quite perilously euphoric, with a sense of physical well-being combined with a zest to catch up with living. Many tensions had vanished. Relationships which had become blurred were passionately renewed or ruthlessly dropped. Decisions were made by emotion rather than by judgement. Lincoln Williams in semi-retirement, after years of specialising in the treatment of alcoholics, was wise on this score. He admitted the possibilities of relapse. "I can allow three. After that, I wash my hands of the patient. Overconfidence is your worst enemy." He was right. I was going about everywhere crying, "Look! No hands!"

Hypnosis formed part of the treatment. I had my doubts about it, claiming that I was too imaginative to become amenable and passive. Both doctors overcame this and Lincoln Williams, in his Brighton sea-front flat, continued to give me hypnotic sessions after the full treatment had finished. We chose the menu. When I was about to appear in Court on a drink charge, which in my view was outrageously unfair, we had Court Behaviour on the menu. I was to be calm, reasonable, not self-assertive and decently repentant. The charge brought by a police officer, on holiday with his family, described my red Renault as a pink Fiat. It stated that I had driven at less than thirty miles an hour and frightened unspecified buses, before parking decorously outside a post office to catch the evening mail. A part of me screamed to attack, but the hypnotic reasonableness of Lincoln Williams had me pleading guilty.

"After all, you say that you didn't have an accident and why should the policeman have followed you for four miles hoping that you would?" Lincoln's quiet voice had urged. "Think of other times when you have driven with too much drink. Aren't you lucky not to have had an accident?" Fortified by this session, I was quite venomously sentenced by a local magistrate who enjoyed every moment of my humiliation. The hypnosis worked. I did not reach for the nearest bottle. I did not even appeal. My inevitable self-pity trip was short.

The effect of hypnosis was, even for me who had never believed in it, stimulating when it set out to be positive and pleasantly sedative at other times. Too sedative, indeed. In hypnotising a patient, Lincoln Williams once hypnotised himself. The two of them remained blithely comfortable, but 'out' to the world throughout a long summer afternoon and evening, emerging refreshed, but somewhat disorientated at dusk.

Lincoln, himself a religious man who went to his death in a fervour of faith, never imposed his beliefs on his patients. He was not explicit about religion but he made it clear, to me at least, that aversion, hypnosis, psychiatry and drugs, the elements of treatment, they were unlikely to be really effective without a spiritual factor. The recovering alcoholic must re-exercise the will to live, must want to live tomorrow, must in fact believe in living. This is where the essential spiritual factor comes in, consolidating the whole operation. Agnostic, Anglican, Jew, Buddhist... Since Lincoln's death, I have seen men and women of every persuasion acknowledging, often with embarrassment, the potency of spiritual grace—or call it just the will to live.

"Never lose that force. Even if you never have a relapse, you may need it." He was right. Ten years after this advice, a decade without drinking or smoking, a catch in my throat was diagnosed as cancer of the oesophagus. One of the legacies of alcoholism, I was told.

Si Dieu n'existait pas, Il faudrait l'inventer

Who invented God for me? I was not born with a knowledge of God or of any supernatural qualities. I was aware first of evil in my mind, my flesh, my actions. This was my small burden of heredity. A scientific as well as a spiritual fact. The logic of Original Sin, which I accept.

So my parents bequeathed this element of sin and, as I became conscious as a human being, they invented God. I do not blame them of course for the inheritance or the creation of the image. My mother and my father were paragons of goodness and innocence compared with myself. Their actual scope for evil was in any case much narrower. Another generation back, it could well have been the other way round. The progression of virtue and vice, in terms of heredity and opportunity—with the exotic emergence of saints or black sheep from time to time—is not an immediate issue with me now, though it may be God controlled. My parents were unaware of, and not responsible for all those basic qualities, which may be, perhaps, too loosely lumped together as heredity. They were aware of the need of God and their responsibility to invent the image of Him for my benefit.

They did not share this task equally. My father regarded it as a woman's job. About religion, he was reticent, staunch, truculent, embarrassed and conventional. Not, of course, simultaneously, but as circumstances demanded. His reticence took the form of never discussing God if it could be avoided. His embarrassment was manifest if anybody did such a thing outside church. His staunchness was revealed in his acceptance of divine power; primarily as a farmer, but also as a gardener, cricketer and rider to hounds. God sent good hay-making weather, soggy cricket pitches, frost in May, bad days for scent. He was truculent if anybody, however innocently, seemed to call God in question. He would say, as he pointed upward, "Of course, God's up there." His conventionality was stressed in his strict adherence to Church of England forms of service, appropriate choice of well-known hymns for the right occasion, timing of sermons, behaviour in church, unostentatious conduct of the rites of baptism, marriage and death. He supported rather than invented God.

My mother was more militant, less inhibited and well aware that it was up to her to confront her only son with God. Her horizons giving access to heaven were wider. She had been brought up in Australia and, in the course of her travels between northern and southern hemispheres, had actually encountered heathens—missionaries too. Later, as a nurse training at the Rotunda, Dublin, she had developed a social conscience which had few other than Anglican outlets in a placid rural community in the first decade of this century. God, for her, was related to good work. She was a steady, but not ostentatious or self-indulgent do-gooder; married to a man who made a virtue of idleness and did not either denigrate or participate in the works of the godly.

For me, my mother lovingly and painstakingly created the image of God as The Old Man in the Sky. He was hirsute, effulgent, tinted royal blue and gold. He was weightless, cloud-borne, yet substantial. His reality emanated from a stained-glass window in the church, where my mother took her turn at doing the flowers. "But it's only a likeness of God, a portrait, John."

Photographs had recently been taken in the family. I asked if this was a photo of God.

"Oh no, John, God can't be photographed."

"Why not?"

"You can't *see* God. And you can't photograph what you can't see."

"Then why do people paint his picture on windows?"

I can't vouch for the exact phrasing of this chilly logic of my extreme youth. I remember though that my mother, probably in some desperation, replied, "They are imagining God. And now, be a good boy and fetch the blue jug from the porch."

God was more immediate than the blue jug. I lingered. This may have been my introduction to poetic licence but I was puzzled. If God was not here or there, to be snapped or to sit for his portrait in a window, where was he? My mother pointed upward and said he was in heaven.

"In the roof?"

"No," she sighed, with a professional nurse's patience. "Far above in the sky." When people painted him on windows they just had to imagine what he was like. They were clever, religious, artistic people and knew what they were doing.

The blue jug in the porch was tangible. The Old Man in the Sky from that moment was real. Hairy, blue and goldish, having his picture painted sometimes on church windows. I was an only child and lacked communication. My thoughts and my talk were bound up with the living things I most loved: a white dog called Barney; Mr Joy the grave-digger, who worked for us when not engaged in his official tasks; his grandson, a ruthless, wonderfully beautiful boy called

SI DIEU N'EXISTAIT PAS, IL FAUDRAIT L'INVENTER

Ginger. Women did not come into it. The only woman was my mother who had, among other things, invented God. I added God to my list. The Old Man in the Sky.

He was not palpable, tangible but solid all through, even if His immediate image was portrayed in the single dimension of stained glass. My mother taught me The Lord's Prayer, my first introduction to formal prayer-making. Though much of it was puzzling or incomprehensible, The Old Man in the Sky fitted into it fairly well. At least it began well by stating that he was everybody's father—the grave-digger's, Ginger's, Barney's, even my own grandfather's. I accepted that, for my mind had not begun to question the mechanics of breeding. The assertion '*art* in Heaven' pleased me, because it was positive and blunt. I tried using the verb *art*. 'Barney art in his kennel,' I would say. But my mother said, vaguely and not too accurately, that it was a word used specially for God. "It's not right to use such words about a little dog, even though we are very fond of him," she explained.

I discovered that there were a great many God-words used to please The Old Man in the Sky in The Lord's Prayer, and indeed in everything that had to do with church-going. It was not necessary to understand them. In fact, it seemed to cause misgivings if one asked questions about them. It sounded good, felt good and pleased everybody—including, I was assured, The Old Man himself—if one just rattled off the prayers in a lilting lisp, words and phrases, beginning, '*Are far which art teven* ...'

There would be promptings of course, but if one reached the end without actually having to go back and start at the beginning, there was praise like, 'What a clever little fellow!' and sometimes something worth having to eat. Nothing came from The Old Man in the Sky. He had his hands full giving out daily bread and forgiving trespasses. Ah yes, and that was the hard word, both to say and to understand. *Tweshpish* was the nearest I got to it. I might have accepted it as a God-word but for the sudden emergence of trespassers upon our modest domain; first in the cherry orchard, then in two of the meadows leaving gates open. They were actual people—and villains at that.

"They trespassers done no end of harm. You should hear the Guvnor. All wrought up, he is. They come off the footpath and through the hedge. Bleedin' nuisance them trespassers."

It was the grave-digger holding forth in the kitchen. Later, it was my father, all wrought up, ordering barbed-wire and a notice that trespassers would be prosecuted.

What about forgiving them? If they were real people who were wicked, and needed barbed-wire to keep them out, why didn't The Old Man in the Sky stop them? And what about our own trespasses? If we didn't do them, why did we ask to be forgiven? In a halting barrage of questions, I taxed my mother with all this. She did her best to explain that trespass as a God-word was quite different from that used for people breaking through the hedge and leaving gates open. I doubt if I got The Lord's Prayer off pat for many years after that. I always stumbled when I came to our *tweshpishes*, my mind wandering to the end of the meadow by the footpath where all the barbed-wire was, together with several notice-boards.

My belief in the God my mother had invented for me held fast so long as the first small world of my innocence stood about me, though from time to time I was assailed by dismay that The Old Man in the Sky did not take a more active part in our lives. Could he not stop the splinter going into my finger, or Ginger's black eye, or the hayrick catching fire? My mother said he had all mankind to think about, the wicked as well as the good, and that pain and trouble were sent to try us.

SI DIEU N'EXISTAIT PAS, IL FAUDRAIT L'INVENTER

"Things don't always turn out as they should," she sighed. "We must just accept His will."

This was puzzling, but I put my own interpretation on it. The Old Man was just too busy. Think of all the daily bread he had to give. No wonder He looked so solemn, so unsmiling.

That view of Him was changed on a sultry day in the hay field. My mother had gone indoors to see about the refreshments which would be brought out to the hay-makers in the little trap drawn by Jenny the Frisky; a pony of very uncertain temper. There were a few heavy sploshes of rain. Then thunder rumbled.

"Don't 'ee be afraid, little John. They be playing football up there above," said Mr Joy, pointing to the curdled sky.

"Is that what they're doing?" I was afraid, reassured and exalted, all in turn.

The thunder rumbled closer. "Ay, seems as if somebody's going to score a goal afore long," laughed Mr Joy.

I laughed too—to show that I was not afraid, and also because I was pleased that they were having a bit of fun up there. *They?* The Old Man was surrounded by angels. They were the ones who would be kicking the ball around. The Old Man might be smiling, enjoying the fun like Grandad at Christmas. He would not be doing the kicking Himself. But at least, I thought, as the thunder quickly passed and the pony trap appeared in the distance, at least something happens up there which we can hear.

"I've had such trouble with Jenny. I thought she was going to bolt because of the thunder," my mother said as she drove up. "You weren't afraid, John?"

"Not a bit afraid. I like to hear God having a game of football."

"Who told you *that* story?" My mother, to whom God was

no joking matter, looked sharply at the grave-digger and Ginger giggled, winking at me.

"I heard them. They were having fun up there," I said, serene in my revelation.

That serenity lasted until I went to school. I was not much given to thought, and my prayers were a matter of routine. The image of The Old Man in the Sky was always there when needed. The conception was as primitive and as well-attended by its simple taboos, as that of any savage tribe, though my mother had no idea of this. She was just content that she had set my feet on the right path. It was straight and narrow all right, but it was also mined. It was Barney, the dog, that sprung the first mine. He died.

He was much older than I was, as everyone pointed out, and he just died of old age. Mr Joy dug a grave of course, and he was buried in a corner of the orchard while I was at school.

I went off my food and lost my power of speech. They did not send me to school the next day, but they were unable to realise that a great part of my world had vanished. They grieved themselves and were sorry that I took it so hard. Then, coaxing me to eat something, my mother said, "Barney will be quite happy where he has gone."

"Where is that?" These were perhaps the first words I had spoken that day. "You buried him in the orchard. Not even in the churchyard."

"Not dogs in the churchyard. It's consecrated ground."

"What sort of ground?"

"I mean a dog isn't a Christian."

"Not even Barney?" I gulped over the name.

"Not a Christian, dear, he was only a dog."

"But he was good."

"And I expect his spirit's gone to a dog's heaven."

"You mean God won't have him?"

SI DIEU N'EXISTAIT PAS, IL FAUDRAIT L'INVENTER

"Just eat up, John, and don't ask any more questions."

"I won't eat unless I know Barney's gone up to The Old Man in the Sky."

"You're getting too old to call him that. Just say God, there's a good boy."

Then I was choking. "God won't have Barney. He's gone somewhere else. I shan't ever see him again."

My mother was patient with me, but her religious scruples would not on any account admit dogs to heaven. Little did she realise that she, in her righteousness, began the destruction of that hairy, blue and goldish figure, The Old Man in the Sky. From that moment, my unquestioning belief in that image began to wane. Soon the God she had invented for me had vanished. His place in the sky was empty.

The Only Child

The sky has remained empty. Manifestations and images of God have appeared on the road rather than above it. Yet often, when I am thanking goodness for cake, I glance at the empty sky, not exactly expectant, but re-enacting for a second the wonder of the myth of The Old Man in the Sky.

An only child can hardly fail to be a loner, through circumstance if not by nature. The environment is triangular—Mum, Dad and Me. Parents concentrating love, concern, admiration or criticism on just the One who must be a credit to them, or perhaps do them proud. The One's virtues and talents, if any, are taken for granted, and are often ascribed as taking after Mum, Dad, Uncle George, some long since dead grandparent or some mythical family trait. The One does not earn much of the credit for being good, yet he bears the full burden of being bad. The only child is at the apex of triangular domestic scrutiny. No brothers and sisters diffuse the shortcomings. He has no witnesses, no confidantes. Upon his narrow shoulders grows the awareness of the two sides of the family.

Mother's side resolutely gentrified, extrovert, travelled, risk-taking, talented, sometimes successful. Father's side resolutely yeoman, socially mixing with neither gentry nor working class, taking no risks, keeping themselves to themselves, fond of telling one another that they were not as young as they were. Aunt May, who most frequently made this remark, lived to run a motor-mower over her grass at the age of ninety-six. Very early on, I became aware of this suppressed conflict, between the two sides. The maternals that you had to live up to; the paternals to whom you must never show off. Through being sent to boarding schools, I acquired a genteel accent which, like a fear of mathematics, I have never been able to throw off. This put me at a distance from the paternals and was taken for granted by the maternals. As the only representative of my generation, I came under family scrutiny which lasted until I ran out of aunts and uncles. When my first marriage broke up, a senior Pudney aunt pursed up her lips. "We have never had a divorce in the family." Since the aunts had never married, and the uncle had been well into middle-age when he took the plunge, the likelihood was remote, but the shame on me was undiminished. When I went public as an alcoholic, writing about it in a Sunday newspaper and appearing in a David Frost television programme, one of the maternal relatives declared, "Of course you aren't any such thing. Our family has never been given to drink. You are only doing it for the money." The idea of labelling yourself an alcoholic in order to wrest a bit of extra money from the media, might seem far-fetched but, where family status seems threatened any excuse is valid. To take money on false pretences was better than being an alcoholic. Such attitudes generate some of the worst problems of over-drink, the social stigma, the secrecy at all costs, the refusal to accept the blemish as an illness.

As the only one of my generation, I was used to some bizarre family comments and to pursed-up silences of disapproval. At least I acquired tolerance with the years. But, in my teens and twenties, I was often hurt, and passively withdrew from family patterns; not wholly, nor aggressively, but creating some degree of defensive isolation.

Isolation I take to be the enemy of the individual, the community and the nation. Whether it be self-imposed or enforced from outside by people or by cicumstance, it is a corrosive evil. In the individual, its commonest and most destructive manifestation is self-pity. When my first marriage was falling apart, I would drive the car quite carefully on a five-hour journey, taking myself through the whole script of my misfortune not only once, but with several repeats. I was intoxicated with self-pity, not alcohol. I made no stops for food or drink and fearfully ignored hitch-hikers. The trance ended with quite copious libations to speed its withdrawal. I was not my own man. I was never more wasted and spent, never more out of communication, never more alone than in such times of self-imposed isolation. Drink was the lubrication.

Now, in my latter years, I am not too good at being alone. I have learnt how precious is communication. Yet I value solitude, which for me is the obverse of isolation in that I seek it and order it, taking advantage of circumstances. I can even choose to share it.

Between these two is loneliness, which wrings my heart whenever I detect it in others. It is the state of needing but failing to communicate. The need may be hard or soft, a barely conscious whisper or demand crying out. Circumstances, environment or age may cause it. Where the isolated one is looking inward, back to the world, blinds drawn, the lonely one is peering out, pathetically, wistfully, brazenly or through the tiniest chink of hope.

While I would not wish it on anyone to be an only child, the picture of deprivation and actual suffering is often luridly overdrawn. In hindsight, I can see some deprivations and moments of actual suffering. At the time I was not aware of anything wrong or not being as it should be. I am still surprised at the stress that some people, not only psychiatrists, lay upon only childhood; seeing in it, for instance, the roots of sexual aberration, lust, impotence, all three. Nearly every undesirable trait I have shown in my lifetime has been attributed by someone to only childhood.

Much depends upon the setting and circumstance, whether the home is open or closed to its environment, and to the stimulus of communication. At Langley, I was born into a rural setting, unaware of all that threatened it. Dogs, horses, Plymouth Rock hens, a mud-banked stream, buttercup meadows, cherry orchards, a blacksmith's forge up the road, labourers about the place, maids who acted as nannies. The people spoiled me, the creatures loved me. I loved everything. When I was lonely, I talked to the nearest human—Father called it stopping people working—to the animals, often to the stream, to one or two orchard trees, and to an oak near the forge which I called Canada, and which was still there—with no trace of the forge, in the 1970s. I also talked to imaginary companions, which unaccountably made some people feel sorry for me, murmuring about missing brothers and sisters.

I did not miss what I had never experienced. I did not feel deprived. I had this self-sufficiency, a natural compensation perhaps, and I was undoubtedly happy in those early pre-school days. I can't believe that those undemanding years in which I was sometimes punished for misdeeds—stealing eggs and fruit, mowing down two rows of broad beans in flower, exposing myself at a flower show—left bruises which survived into manhood. Rather, I believe that the magic wonder of cake found its place in my nature, not baked or initialled by any of the people I loved, but as integral and lasting as my navel.

Such was the setting. Until World War I came and I went to school, I had not realised that the family environment was so circumscribed, the communication so limited; or that

London, always spoken of with awe as something alien, was only seventeen miles away. This proximity was brought home to me when my mother was cherry-picking and I was assisting from a few rungs down the ladder, and we heard rumbling across the tree tops to the east. "Listen!" my mother said. "That's a German air raid on London. What a good thing we live in the country."

"Shall we see the Zeppelins?" I wondered.

"London is much too far away, John."

Throughout my youth, 'going up to town' was a breathtaking event, requiring a day's preparation. Before I was out of my teens, I was a season-ticket holder.

Awareness of being an only child came with the first school. It was not a sense of deprivation through lack of brothers and sisters. Schoolboys, in my experience, are generally reticent about their siblings. It was then I perceived that my fellows, even though some of them were sons of Slough trades people who called for orders, enjoyed a more open environment. Slough in those days was not a town of vivid cultural or social attraction. Yet it seemed to me that these other boys were more favoured, more sophisticated (it would be a decade before I would use such a word) more sociable, more outgoing than I, emerging from my remote rusticity just two and a half miles away. I felt myself to be an outsider, a perpetual junior, the first effects of only childhood.

It made me by turns competitive and withdrawn. At my prep school, I became head boy. At Gresham's, I had a happy but hopeless career, passing no exams, gaining no distinctions. On leaving prematurely, however, to start work in a London estate agency, I took postal tuition and went to night school and passed without hitch all the professional exams, which included such subjects as Drainage and Sanitation. I had my first poems and articles published. Having dodged or slacked at games at school, I became a rugger fanatic and captained a side at Windsor. I organised lurid little dances for the younger office staff in a basement in the then drab Carnaby Street. I was the 'life and soul' of the juniors. Beer flowed copiously. The prestige of being a lusty drinker was consolidated with boastful hangovers. This feverish social and sporting activity, reassured by beer, was compensating for only childhood. It was accompanied by headlong pursuit of girls, a dazzling novelty, an endless fiesta of promiscuity with highlights of calf-love and quite rare moments of fulfilment. Nothing at home or at school had prepared me for this. I had no difficulty in finding girls. I had not been warped by only childhood. Perhaps I was over-compensating. Perhaps feeling myself the only one of my generation made me extra randy. Meanwhile, the writing of poetry, stories and articles went on defiantly in solitudes of their own. My father's family was derisive; my mother's family feared a Bohemian streak. Only a few of my boon companions knew of these clandestine labours. When something was published in *Country Life*, the office bosses began to wonder if I were 'really heart and soul in the job', which was the bizarre standard they set for juniors who got free articles of indenture, but neither time off nor expenses for sweating through the professional exams. I had doubts myself which I shall mention later. The competitive pack-leading, over-stimulation of my late teens, was surely a manifestation of only childhood. The astonishing thing is that some form of creative writing, not exceptional, certainly lacking quality, kept going and gained ground.

The other side of my teenage nature, of which I was unaware until later and which persists to this day, is withdrawal, distrust, wariness and an almost hysterical need to measure myself against people. This is little Johnny, peering out from the circumscribed world of boyhood and the solitary vantage points on the paths that led away from it. When I went to Gresham's School as a new boy, after lording it at the old-fashioned rather cosy prep school—one of the masters hunted and it was one of my perks to act as groom—I was humanely welcomed and taken for a bicycle ride by a good Quaker Rowntree, then head of the House. In spite of such liberal treatment and general lack of intimidation, I went quiet. I made no effort to give out anything, to anyone. I was the dullest new boy in anyone's memory. The death of my mother during my second term accentuated this withdrawal. In less than a year, though, I had found friends, formed a gang and, socially at least, prospered. But I remained in my heart a junior boy, non-competitive, conventionally eccentric, immersed in Norfolk countryside writing, and enjoying very pure romantic friendships. Not in any aspect of life ambitious, just adding to the early only childhood experience, reverting in many ways to it. There was no snobbery about; yet I had been acquiring the accents and the attitudes of the Gent and I had misgivings. The maternal side of the family was satisfied 'so long as I *behaved* like one'. The paternal side had suspicions about the boy giving himself airs for my father spoke with a warm countrified accent which I came to admire more and more as I grew older.

This going quiet, regressing to childhood wonder, awareness of immaturity sometimes rewarded with cake, went on throughout the years; not always an asset on the face of it, but I now discover it was not by any means a disadvantage. Over-drink would have mastered me completely without it.

Obviously it immediately afflicted me on leaving school and going straight into a big office, 'starting at the bottom' where a Gent's accent and attitudes were targets for mockery and humiliation for long miserable winter months; until I surprised myself and everyone else by breaking out of it and getting some laughs.

I did not always break out in after life. The junior boy feeling crept over me for instance when I became a member of the Savile Club, which I enjoyed for some twenty years without feeling that I belonged to the sixth form—in spite of playing so much squash with Stephen Potter while he was creating gamesmanship. I had the same feeling, but with less enjoyment, for many years at the Press Club.

Joining the staff of the BBC in the thirties, I was indeed a junior, though not starting at the bottom—I never did that again. The only excuse for it is sheer necessity. First, I had to learn how to work on the editorial staff of *The Listener*, then my incompetence promoted me to programme production, where I had to learn everything overnight. This was the ludicrously under-staffed, overworked and recklessly cheerful beginning of the Empire Programmes which was a pioneering wonder of the world Overseas Programmes.

In those days, nearly everyone at Broadcasting House had started work somewhere else at some other kind of job. The generation of those brought up within the Corporation had not got under way. So people were kind about my inexperience, though I did not chat it around that I had been a rent collector in Soho. But educational background of a very high order was taken for granted. 'I don't remember which college you were at. Perhaps it wasn't Oxford, but the other place?' Such was the amicable conversational balloon which would float toward me over morning coffee. I learnt to shoot it down by saying: 'I'm just self educated.' It worked well but the junior boy inhibition always lingered.

Joining the RAF—as an officer, no more starting at the bottom—a worm's eye sense of juniority went with the first posting. I was pushed around. I was approaching thirty, a father, author of three or four books. That maturity bit did not sustain me. I was just regarded as *old*. The same sensation loomed over each new posting, and I went quiet and stayed quiet, taking it all in. Then there was a sudden rush of confidence. The RAF was a way of life to which one belonged, shyly and rather derisively creating loyalties, as in a lesser degree the stint in the BBC had done. I met the sixth-formers at all rank levels, liked them and yet felt withdrawn from them.

It is significant that some success in each of these environments seemed to me to need regular steady and wonderfully convivial alcoholic support—support which had vanished by the following day.

I once met George Bernard Shaw at the Maddox Street Exhibition, where the pictures of D. H. Lawrence, subsequently seized by the police, were on view. When somebody culture-thirstily enquired at a dinner in Cairo during the war, "What sort of a man is he?" I said, "Well, he doesn't smoke or drink." I paused and got my laugh. I was ashamed. The shame was drowned. That's the sort of help you get.

Names

Going on and back from George Bernard Shaw, I concede that Names dropped in any autobiographical work are an invitation, and Names dragged in are an insult to the reader. I venture, perhaps recklessly, to shepherd relevant ones into a single corral.

They are those I met: as a feature writer on a national newspaper, in the course of business, under my own flag, and as a fellow writer. The journalistic interviews counted for nothing. I was not myself; merely a man from the *News Chronicle*. Noël Coward paid me more attention than the others at his press conference because I was still rather pretty. Rachmaninoff, travel-weary from the last century as well as this, closed his eyes as if it were the millionth press conference, which it probably was, and became an event rather than a person. Probably I asked the same sort of idiot questions that interviewers peel off on television in the seventies.

Under my own flag, I met Picasso, Winston Churchill, Dwight Eisenhower, Charles Chaplin, without one of these remembering so much as my name after I had bowed out. Each encounter gave me a little, however.

Picasso, I 'liberated' in Paris in 1944. He was walking down to the door of the block of mansion flats where he had an apartment, and he was accompanied by a large, graceful, closely-clipped, grey dog. He was on the point of taking his first more or less peaceful walk along the Seine to his studio off the Boulevard St Michel.

His hand was warm, his greeting was quick; the great dark eyes were as vivid as ever. Five years of war had not cast any physical shadow upon the prophet painter of Guernica. "It will be more amusing," he said, "if we talk in my studio—and you can see what I have been up to." So we climbed the circular, shambling wooden stairs toward the studio, which Picasso said he had always had in Paris. There was a hall littered with books. Then came a large room, 'a little of a factory and something of a studio'. Picasso pointed with his foot lightly toward a Matisse. There were other pictures belonging to my host, a superb Douanier Rousseau, for example. There were no works by Picasso.

But at last we began to talk about the closed years; and Picasso with his fine hands and long regular finger-nails, smiled with his eyes. He turned from the works of other men and beckoned me to follow him up one more staircase. "I have worked on," he said. "They would not let me exhibit, but I worked and all my work is here." We came into a working studio perched amid the Montparnasse roofs, so recently— and still occasionally—battlegrounds for snipers. This studio was packed with four years' work of Picasso.

I forget how it was ranged, how one looked at it. There was no order, just sufficient orderliness. During all the closed years, Picasso had never ceased to work in this studio. As the horror once seen at Guernica extended over the face of the earth, Picasso had worked with undiminished zeal. He believed that outside events caused him to seek a greater objectivity. He said that the tendency in the creative artist is to stabilize mankind on the verge of chaos. Talk went like that, not using many words, but referring from time to time to the collection of pictures not yet enjoyed by the critics of the free world. There was a series of almost representational paintings of the Seine, on and about the Ile St Louis—nearly the most hackneyed landscape in Paris. There were four very exact likenesses of a boy model, drawn during this summer of war. There were a number of drawings of the pot of growing tomatoes which stood in the window, and at least two finished paintings had those same tomatoes as a central theme.

"A more disciplined art, less unconstrained freedom, in a time like this is the artist's defence and guard," Picasso said. "Very likely for the poet it is a time to write sonnets. Most certainly it is not a time for the creative man to fail, to shrink, to stop working. Think of the great poets and painters of the Middle Ages."

We looked at larger canvases, at painting lighter, gayer, but as strong and free as the pre-war works I had known. Not being competent to write of painting, I have no words either in French or in English with which to praise or to examine such things. Picasso showed me the more recent, and he pointed out the significance of the dates. There stood the big picture finished on 19 August 1944, when the fighting started. There were sketches dated day by day during the battle of Paris. On 24 August, when Tiger tanks were fighting round the corner in the Boul Mich, when Germans and French Fascists were fortified in the Luxembourg, when the Prefecture just across the river on the Ile de la Cité was a strongpoint, Picasso glanced at a work by Poussin. As the windows rattled with the fighting, he began copying Poussin's design. "It was an exercise, a self-discipline, a healthy fascination." He worked at it throughout the loud, angry days of the liberation on 25 August 1944.

Now the sun shone upon the much-painted tomato plant, and Paris was quiet. One must see the rest of the studio apartment, the cool Spanish tiled floor of the bedroom, the bathroom with twin wash-hand basins, 'either a hand in each, or an intelligent conversation with a friend while you wash'. In the littered hall again, Picasso displayed the savage literature of the enemy. He had quietly collected the Nazi and collaborationist periodicals in which his own work had been attacked. His remarkable hands turned over the pages which reproduced his work. *Picasso the Jew ... the decadent Pablo Picasso ... the obscene pornographer* ... went the captions. "And now, at least, that is at an end," he said, simply allowing for one moment that relief, which all intellectual Paris was expressing, to show itself in his own face.

Before I left, I enquired if there was anything Picasso needed immediately, besides the cigarettes which I had brought. His only request was modest enough. He showed me the worn wafer of soap which was the butt of his shaving-stick. I thought of that legion of would-be painters whose beards testified to their aspirations, and I thought of the master with the thousands of pounds' worth of painting upstairs, who required only the means to shave. It was one of the war's less worthy paradoxes; but it amused both of us, standing there at the threshold of sunny, free Paris. Then he thanked me gravely and did not ask my name. I came away enriched by the powerful serenity of the man, the glorious indifference.

Earlier that year, the forthcoming invasion of Europe brought me into the presence of Ike, who could be said to have had a remarkable load on his mind. The RAF was sending me as special observer, working with the American and Allied Forces as well as our own. The great man was countersigning my special pass. Why it was thought necessary for me to interview him, or be briefed by him, I never could discover and he, though he clearly knew more than most people about the conduct of the war, was unclear on the point. He nonplussed me by addressing me as John, and asked where I came from. "Malta," I said, guessing that he couldn't mean my home town. He showed interest but talked on the telephone (perhaps to God?). He was very crisply laundered. What on earth could I tell him about Malta that he would want to know? He saved me by putting down the telephone to dismiss me with the words "Well, good luck, Jimmy."

I came away enriched by the neat security of the man in a climate of nail-biting. Nice to learn in the Sunday papers, some decades afterwards, that he was also in love.

In the 1945 General Election, I contested Tory Sevenoaks for Labour and naturally lost. I lived with my first wife and young family in Westerham Valley and, because we were friends with Christopher and Mary Soames, we were sometimes invited to use the Chartwell pool in the post-war years.

"So you are the poet fellow who came and canvassed my Chartwell staff for Labour?" What do you say to Sir Henry Newbolt?

He stood in his great toga-like bath-robe, and misquoted excruciatingly from my favourite jingo poet. I nodded and shivered appreciatively, wishing my own towel was within reach.

"When do you propose to try again? You're the right age."

I said I didn't think I could afford another go. It was difficult for a writer.

"But I'm a writer," he thundered. "I don't care which side you're on. Talent is what is wanted."

I came away impressed by his generosity.

A few miles away at Sidney Bernstein's farm in the Weald, I met Charlie Chaplin, who made no concessions to ranch-style gear and was wearing a blue business suit rather shiny round the backside. He was about to promote *Limelight* and was looking over his native land trying to establish the good things. I suppose it was with the idea of establishing realities, that we went to a modest hedgerow pub down the road—incognito of course. A desultory stand-about of customers passed the time of day and endless platitudes took over. The sweet innocence of the country local drugged senses, until I went to the outside Gents and saw the cars streaming in. The bush telegraph of Kent had been prodigiously active. The very ordinary little man in the blue city suit was already besieged by autograph paper, pints of beer, and pleas to put on his bowler or do a funny walk.

After the rescue, there was silence between us which made me uneasy.

"I didn't tip them off," I said.

"I'm sure you didn't." He glanced at his watch—or was it mine? "We'd better be getting along. They'll be wondering where we are ..."

I came away realising, not for the first time, that funny men are not funny, but they make secret demands for protection or affection which are irresistible.

Donald Maclean is hardly a matching name, but he's a fine notoriety. I had known him slightly at Gresham's School and when Patrick Kinross, who knew him quite well, was staying with us in Kent and suggested inviting him and Melinda for Sunday morning drinks, I teased him about the old school circuit and agreed. I was deep in the fleshpots of the fifties, writing hectically in order, I told myself, to bring up a family, but also to eat and drink too much. I was well on with a novel called *The Net* and should have spent the Sabbath in my hut at the bottom of the garden finishing the penultimate chapter. Instead, I sat with Donald finishing the Booth's gin, ready to go across to the pub opposite for more.

"What are you writing at this moment?"

"A novel," I said. "It came to me after a job I was doing among the research people at the Royal Aeronautical Establishment at Farnborough. It's about treachery ... or perhaps that's not the word ... defection. A Farnborough type of scientist taking off and offering himself and his bag of tricks to Russia."

How often have I gone back over that in vain searching my memory for some trace of tension, some catch of breath, any indication at all that this was Donald's last Sunday in Kent. When we telephoned to invite the pregnant Melinda to tea the next day or the day after, a CID voice came on the line. Then we read about it in the papers. It made the closing chapters of *The Net* singularly difficult to write, with this bizarre truth breathing down the neck of fiction.

I never did seek out literary celebrities. I claim that in my favour. It must have been several years after I left school before I ever met an established author. Many of my school fellows were at university while I drudged about delivering letters by hand, working the hydraulic lift, licking stamps at fifteen shillings a week, the starting at the bottom which was sacred to my paternalistic employers. ('To our happy family,' the honoured toast at every annual dinner.) This feeling of missing out on the gentlemanly, leisurely, and, as I imagined, cultured life at a university, formed a chip on my shoulder which I have never been able to laugh off. It had a powerful reverse angle. For when I met some of these privileged contemporaries, they seemed still to be boys, and myself, particularly after I had been entrusted with some Soho rent collections, to be a man of the world. That was only a passing satisfaction. My own writing, very juvenile and doddery, went on, not secretly but unobtrusively. I was resolute enough but weighed down with diffidence, very much the junior boy again. I didn't yearn for the company of writers, I never have.

But I made Soho friends unconnected with my job.

Then within the space of a year or so, after turning twenty, things opened out. I was courting my first wife Crystal, daughter of A. P. Herbert, I had playlets broadcast, poems published in a first slim volume. The Herbert social circle was studded with celebrities, but there was a generation gap and we, contentedly, played along as juniors with a good measure of precocity. The publication of my book was followed by an almost regal summons, via the publisher, to attend a Thursday tea party at the salon of Lady Ottoline Morrell. So much has been written about the formidable Ott, too much of it ungenerous. I loved her for her generosity and forthrightness; taking me because she liked those first poems, and unfailing afterwards with sharp-edged advice. Her emphasis was always on quality and I wish I had heeded her more.

I stole time from the office to attend that first Thursday summons. A severe maid answered the door in Gower Street and announced me to the tea-table.

The Ott stood swaying and growling. "Mr Pudney has a new book of poetry out. Now ..." She introduced the table, "Mr W. B. Yeats, Mr James Stephens, Mr Eliot ..." There were three or four more whose names I was too stunned to catch.

Her husband, Philip Morrell, said helpfully "We were discussing Jane Austen at this end of the table. How does she stand to a writer of your generation?"

To me, she was just an Eng. Lit. item at school. She was not to come into my life until some years later—in a tent in the Western Desert of all places.

I looked wild-eyed at the benign courtly figure of Philip Morrell, who read the panic signal and instantly released me. "But we mustn't spoil your tea. Do have a cucumber sandwich."

NAMES

It was the custom to move into the drawing-room overlooking Gower Street gardens after tea. The guests were spaced about and judiciously moved. I was led to a small sofa, where there was enough of a ledge to sit beside the ample sprawl of W. B. Yeats—like perching on the edge of the lap of God.

"So you have a book out?"

This was fame. Even God himself knew about my book. He sighed and added, "What do you do?"

How could I tell this God-poet whose work had illuminated my life, that I was collecting rents and trying to let places?

"Well, of course I try to write ..." I began.

"That doesn't keep you in bread and butter."

I told him I had filled in an application for the BBC and that I was trying publishing. He denounced both in measured, indeed weighty terms which thudded down on my senses. Then as the Ott, with her immaculate timing, swooped to rescue me, he said, "Your place, young man, is in the theatre."

I only met him once again—and it was in Tottenham Court Road. I had been instructed to let the upper floors of the Montague Burton building on the corner of New Oxford Street, next to the Dominion Theatre. It was so important that I was told to equip myself with a small office on the spot. Leaving this one evening, I found myself face to face with Yeats, who stood outside the Dominion Theatre gazing across the road towards the building with the Guinness clock at the end of Oxford Street. I was carrying a measuring rod and several rolls of floor plans. I was wearing a bowler hat. Though I revered Yeats more than almost any other living man, I tried to side-step. But he made a great wide gesture, beckoning me to his side. Though his gaze seemed fixed above the Guinness clock, he had instantly recognised me in my hesitation and called me by name. There was no escape.

"I am contemplating the fairies," he said, in a portentous voice.

I had reason to know that there were fairies about on these pavements, but he gripped my arm and pointed to the rooftops. "You can hardly fail to see them, young man. They are dancing above the Guinness clock," he declared. "I always stop at this place and watch them."

While I kept my temporary office in that building, I sometimes went to the window in the later afternoon to be rewarded by a view of Yeats, standing solitary like a great untidy statue, jostled by unconcerned people grabbing evening papers, as he watched the roof fairies above the Guinness clock. When I mentioned this to The Ott, she purred loud. "What a privilege to share the vision. I must look out for him at the bus-stop."

For me, the magic of the man diminished. I would never seek out his presence. He would become less a God than a curiosity. But his poetry held its sway. I had learnt once and for all that contact with a creative person should have no effect on one's appreciation of his creative work. The most glamorous people, whose company could be so rewarding, were quite likely to produce boring or pretentious work.

The prose writer who affected me most deeply, whose simplicity and directness I envied and admired above all, was Ernest Hemingway. Just before D-Day 1944, I was at Gravesend with Peter Wykeham, who was commanding a Mosquito Wing doing a pre-invasion harassment of German lines of communication along the French coast. We were tense. Casualties were heavy. The quality of replacements left something to be desired. "We have Ernest Hemingway doing his bit of front line reporting," Peter told me. "I'll do what I can, but you must do a lot of filling in. Lucky break for you, in fact."

Lucky break indeed! My encounter with the great man began with instant dislike and it ended in a drunken blur of grief that such a fellow should be such a peerless craftsman in words. Hemingway, in his war correspondent's gear, much belted and heavily booted, swaggered about the place acting tough, so tough that it was like some third-rate actor acting Hemingway tough. There was much talk of women and brandy to reinforce the awful impression. The young pilots, keyed up to another heavy night, dried up when he spoke to them, shifted away and enquired in whispers who the character was. Few of them had had time to read Hemingway. They were facing death, but nobody of course spoke of that. The self-centred tough guy histrionics of Hemingway stood out in repulsive contrast in such company. I have read and re-read his work since, admiration untarnished.

The Names I have mentioned were not of my generation. Those who belong to my own time have frightened me much more. Writing is such a solitary, anti-social activity that there often goes with it a craving to belong, to form a circle or even join a club, to be reassured or stimulated by the presence of fellow writers. The Russians were strong on this; Turgenev, Tolstoy, Dostoyevsky always in touch, even if it was to indulge in furious rows. I have briefly experienced the literary coterie in operation; in the thirties in Warsaw, and in the immediate post-war years in Dublin—both communities small enough so that writers could not fail to recognise one another. In the thirties in London there was none of that for my generation in their twenties. A galaxy of writers and pseuds formed round dotty, generous David Archer's bookshop in Parton Street. I first met Dylan Thomas there. But the influential poets, Auden, Spender, Day Lewis, Macneice and Michael Roberts were more a critical grouping which became a sort of literary clique, having no territorial claims. Indeed, Auden—from Keswick—wrote one of his admonitory letters on this point:

"The problem is particularly bad in a city like London, which is so large that the only group you can find is living with your own kind, those mentally like you. This is disastrous, you end up by hating each other. The whole value of a group is that its constituents are as diverse as possible, with little consciously in common, plurality in unity.

"There are some, poets are generally such, who will always be a little outside the group; critical, but they need the group to feel a little out of just as much as the rest need it to be at home in. They get more from it than they know. Without it, they have no material, must split their emotions into even finer hairs."

He continued in a more romantic vein.

"What I feel inclined to say is, Chuck all this literary business. Go and do something useful, like learning to say *I'm very ordinary*, and one day perhaps it'll all come back to you. He who loses his life doth find it. The *litterateur* is as useless to society as a collar stud to a nude woman."

Even before this onslaught, some native shrewdness, some whisper from the old yeoman Pudneys who farmed in East Anglia, had passed the message about being ordinary, not romanticising in the Auden manner but taking a deep breath and looking round in wonder and, yes, finding cake.

I think I was about twenty-five when I first said—more or less to myself—that I was quite a good second-rate poet. I repeated it aloud in a *Guardian* interview in 1976, and some people thought I was a coy old thing. But that assessment, which I suppose I should have kept to myself, has not inhibited my writing the stuff as and when it comes. This is the mystery. You have to wait, and endure periods of dearth—my longest was ten years—and then not only recognise the moment, but have the tools rustless and ready. A moment—minutes or hours—when total relaxation coincides with total concentration.

The poet must be ordinary in that he shares the stresses and jobs of everyday life with his community of neighbours, work people, family old and young. There is need for chosen solitude, not for any ivory tower. Isolation is the enemy. No amount of drink will induce the moment of creation for it is a moment of wonder, of discovery of dangerous innocence. With drink anaesthetising the sensibilities at the front of the brain, there is no wonder, no dangerous innocence. The ghost of doomed Dylan Thomas, from time to time my boon companion, encountered on the dusty stairs avoiding the elevator at the Chelsea Hotel, New York, blurped this truth and sent me scurrying in panic for Alka Seltzer and Vitamin B. I didn't wait to hear his ghostly laughter mocking such palliatives.

Dylan I knew before and after he became famous. He was splendid, rapacious, demanding as a young man. Too much has been written about him for me to add to the legend. As that legend began to grow in his lifetime, I learned to separate him from his poetry, to find him in person increasingly tedious and his poems increasingly exciting, both in print and when he was reading them.

Wystan Auden was a deeper rooted affair. At Gresham's School, during his last term, he fell in love with me and said so very decorously—we still addressed each other by our surnames. It meant that he threw my Swinburne out of the window, lectured me about homosexuality and self-abuse, and took me out to illicit teas. To me, he was an awe-inspiring adult and I wondered that he never touched me. We were in separate houses and our only contacts were long rambling walks which for me were totally magical, even though he took some pains to tell me I was not any good as a poet. To him, I was something pretty and responsive, to be cradled with ideas and affection. A year or so later, he regretted in a letter that we had not had the courage to make a physical thing of it, which suggests that he was, for all the talk, without experience at the time.

Some of the work in the 1930 paperback *Poems* (Faber 2/6d), which made his wide reputation, had been written and read to me at school. The volume itself made a greater impact on me than any work before or since. The tattered, thumbed text is still treasured not only for itself, but as a symbol of some magic, bright, quick, hard, which illuminated the autumn sky in my twenty-first year. The following year, Auden himself made a very different impact. He was staying in London and wrote me a note asking me for my photograph. I was not in my first innocence. I shared attic quarters off Carnaby Street with a fellow clerk and a lady across the landing, a solicitor's daughter from Wiltshire, who was a very professional whore. She sometimes returned off the beat in time to offer us an early morning cup of tea. No man ever came back to her pink-scented room. In spite of this degree of sophistication, I was thoughtlessly flattered to be taken notice of by the poet whose words seemed to be flowing in my veins (causing me to write appalling juvenilia about pylons and tractors).

Of course, as any contemporary reader will have guessed, he wanted to see if I had grown up pretty—and, in the hands of a German photographer, I had. When he came round, there were no concessions to love. It was just meat he was after.

Our acquaintance dwindled into informality after that. When I was on the BBC, I daringly commissioned him to write a programme on Hadrian's Wall, with Benjamin Britten composing and conducting the music. We had a few days together in Newcastle. Benjamin, who was thought by my superiors to be too young for the job, tamed a miners' choir. I became aware that both of them belonged to that homosexual world which closed certain doors to strangers. And, though I might be bisexual from time to time, I would always be a stranger. Auden then drifted right out of my field of vision, though his poetry stayed. Benjamin remained a friend for some years, with a war encounter which I shall mention later, and stood godfather to my son. But from the beginning he was a sixth-former.

The junior boy inhibition is both a safeguard and a tiresome habit of diffidence; a useful curb on pride but easy to slop over into self-pity and isolation. I shrank away from my own generation of poets. I was embarrassed at the prospect of public readings of poetry in their presence. Only in more recent years have I found a kind of freedom in the company of younger writers belonging to a generation more direct, articulate and ruthless. In my late fifties and sixties, I have enjoyed and endured a stimulus and cross-fertilisation which was lacking in my twenties. In the middle years, relationships were blurred; that self-pity and diffidence were always lurking, measuring up everybody, submerged in conviviality, the soft music of expense accounts, the pursuit of quantity instead of quality. In those dear distraught middle years, every success and every misfortune called for its tipple. Turkish baths became a part of the garnishing and it was in the old Imperial that I tried to make my own Name.

Arnold Bennett used to declare, after rendering his favourite song about 'sucking cider through a straw', that he liked to carry a clean five-pound note about with him in London to give to the first person he saw reading one of his books. At that time, when he was still in good voice, he had never parted with any note at all, and his genial advice to the young was never to fall into such a 'foolish state of self-regard'.

Though I hasten to draw no parallels between Arnold Bennett and myself, I was more fortunate than he in this one respect. After celebrating the publication of my book *The Smallest Room*, an essay upon closets and their uses, I decided to propitiate the goddess Cloacina at the Imperial. There, relaxing in nude anonymity in an outer chamber, I closed my eyes and indulged private vanity by wondering what people would make of my book.

Men, wearing brief towelling loin cloths, padded to and fro in that dreamy, steamy nether region where anybody might be anybody. My thoughts reverted to boyhood patterns. Bet they've never written books. Bet they'll wish they'd written *The Smallest Room*. Bet they don't know I wrote it. Opening my eyes to escape from this indulgence, I found myself staring at the well-nourished pink body of a man in a deck chair like mine engrossed in a book—my own.

Engrossed? This was no dream. Though his face was expressionless, his eyes were open. From time to time he turned a page. I began to watch him with obsessive intentness. He never smiled; but neither did he yawn. Vanity broke over me like the sweat of the innermost, hottest room. What chapter could he be reading? Surely not Chapter II, which the publisher and I had optimistically agreed might be considered funny? I could sit still no longer. I rose to make what I hoped would seem a casual circuit. As I approached the back of his chair and made ready to look over his shoulder, however, he shifted impatiently, closed the book on his thumb and moved off to sit on a long bench against the wall.

I went to a water fountain near the bench, sipped and splashed about, going on tiptoe to crane over his shoulder; but he was holding the book at the wrong angle. I pretended, then, to read an evening paper, telling myself that it did not really matter what page he was on so long as he was actually reading my book. Vanity, however, lived and kicked. I simply could not bring myself to lose this conscientious reader for ever in a cloud of steam, without knowing who or what he was, or even what he looked like in his clothes.

I lost control then. I found myself sitting beside him on the bench fatuously remarking, "It's quite warm in here, isn't it?"

"Of course it is! It's meant to be." Once more the book snapped shut, this time without his thumb as a marker. He looked hard at me, seemed to decide that I was harmless, rose to his feet, gave himself a long drink of cold water, then settled down again with the book on a distant bench.

Rebuffed as I was, this new sense of assiduity numbed all sense of propriety. A sort of tenderness intoxicated me as I stared at him, pleased when he sometimes raised his eyes and glared back, but grudgingly, for he was wonderfully deep in the book.

I was in a sort of trance when I made my next move. Determined that sooner or later he should know that I was the author, yet judging that to declare myself in so many words was too bald even in that naked place, I flopped down beside him and, with redoubled fatuity, declared, "Do you find that an interesting book?"

"Of course I do; otherwise I wouldn't be reading it." This time he had had enough. His slamming of the book, his suspicious glare and no-nonsense posture he assumed when he jumped to his feet, brought me to myself. He did not speak, but his very stance was an accusation which cried aloud: "Another word from you and I'll bring a charge ..."

Places

Since my birth at Homewood Farm, Langley and the adjacent market town of Slough have suffered every conceivable social change that this century can inflict upon communities. They are now administratively one. It is a flat stretch of country, part of the alluvial valley of the Thames. Its horizons were often shaped by elms. It is much favoured by rose-growers, nurserymen and, in my early youth, by market-gardeners. The old London to Bath highway runs between it and the Thames. The canal builders excavated from Paddington across Langley to Slough. The incomparable I. K. Brunel ran his Great Western Railway parallel to highway and canal. His first locomotives were barged to West Drayton, assembled and tested on the track down to Langley. In the summer of 1842, Brunel himself was on the footplate of the locomotive, drawing Queen Victoria on her first railroad trip from Slough past Langley Church to the Metropolis, 'free from dust and crowd and heat, and I am quite charmed with it'.

The railway brought season-ticket holders, Horlicks Malted Milk to Slough and good outlets for the local fruit and veg. The canal brought smouldering refuse from West London. The old Bath Road, with its capacious coaching inns, brought through traffic. These communications left village and market town living on in the nineteenth century. My father attended Slough market every Tuesday. Families had their rented pews in Langley Church. There was a large shrub and rose nursery in the main street of Slough. Rough shooting and beagling took place on the ground between the Bath Road and the railway which, at the end of the First World War, became known as the Slough Dump, ultimately becoming the Slough Trading Estate.

It was the Dump which changed the face of things. My father said he would never take a horse near the Bath Road again. I was forbidden to approach it on my bicycle. For, thundering down from London and the ports came the war vehicles, repatriated from the Western Front. They careered along, hard-tyred, in fours. One 'good' one with a smaller one mounted on it, towing a dud carrying a smaller dud. They lurched and swayed past Langley, through Slough, and were ranged acres and acres of them where the beagling and rough shoot had been. There was plenty of caked Flanders mud to be seen. Was there perhaps blood? With a boy from school called Bernard, who had been born in India and had once seen a dead man, a long and hazardous bicycle trip was made. We slid through some fencing near the GWR and spent an hour trying to identify bloodstains. We were seen off by a whiskered khaki figure, looking like Bairnsfather's Old Bill, who was showing people round. Bernard said that it was rather a pity that we had missed the war. That regret lingered for a year or so, after which it went dead. Grown-ups talked about it too much. It belonged to them.

The clearance of the Slough Dump, which took several years, had a national as well as a local effect. The road transport industry started with the men who brought their war gratuities to purchase one or two good trucks and enough bits and pieces to establish a transport business. So the vehicles from the Dump were scattered throughout the country to fight the railway system. Casualties were heavy, many gratuities were lost, but long and short haul road transport became a reality.

As the trucks disappeared, industry came to Slough; and from there, ribbon development along the course of the railway and the canal to Langley. During the twenties and early thirties, workers from every part of the British Isles, particularly the so-called distressed areas, flocked to the new factories. Urbanisation and suburbanisation seeped, spread and congealed with multiple stores and cinemas over the pleasant, flat, undistinguished landscape, leaving a few green pockets of rural life. You did not know everybody any more. People did not know one another or the family connections. Gossip died; veiled disapproval took its place. The last vestiges of the bad old class system were overtaken with status symbolism. Carriage lamps went up. Motor-cars mattered. The authorities named some of the new streets in built-up Langley after notable families who had had pews in the church. I confess to driving round the new labyrinths looking for a stake in posterity called Pudney Crescent, but I guess we were never freeholders and did not qualify for the honour.

The Second World War brought an airfield to Langley and I stepped out of a Mosquito on to land my Uncle George had been farming only a few years before. This would not have been so remarkable—it could happen in any village in Southern England—but for the fact that all trace of aviation had vanished when I made a nostalgic visit a few years after the war. Langley had been right through aviation and had come out on the other side, manufacturing *inter alia* Ford motor-cars. No surprise to be confronted by a singularly purposeless, high-rise block where the Jersey cows used to stare at the testing of prototype aircraft. Among the few green islands left was Homewood, my birthplace, stuffed with busy people, derelict cars and every sort of bird and animal, with a frieze of factories on the skyline beyond the cherry orchards.

To the south, where the motorway junction throws off a tangle of subsidiaries, the old Bath road for one, of course, there was a farm and land familiar to my childhood which remained intact, indeed isolated by highway development. As I came to write these words in the nineteen seventies, this green island had been obliterated by water, a vast reservoir where my son Jeremy, an itinerant champion in International Fourteen Dinghies, sails at weekends. He announced one day, "This race I won on Sunday was at your birthplace."

Why do I still dwell on these despoiled landscapes, which have been so profitable to real estate dealers and offer so little which has distinction or quality? One must not neglect other qualities. It is more productive, more hygienic, more democratic, and perhaps even happier than when I first ran away from it. I was born there in another age—with King Edward VII still on the throne. During my early upbringing, the transformation had already begun. When I started work in London just before my seventeenth birthday, I was already hankering to get away from Langley. I have never had a feeling of roots there. As soon as I went away to boarding school, first on the North Downs, above Westerham, afterward at Holt in north Norfolk, I became aware of and in love with real country which poor doomed Langley, I realised, had never been. From my first journey into London to work, I became ambivalent. I always enter London with relish and leave it to go into the country with a keen sense of anticipation. Much of the time I managed to keep a foothold in both. Writing these words in Greenwich, in an old house which makes the best of both worlds, with a prolific vegetable garden just four and a half miles from Piccadilly Circus, I still keep a bolt-hole on a Sussex farm, where the owner farms on horseback and has never been to London in his life.

Nevertheless, it is Langley which more than any other

place has come into my work, fiction and poetry. I know nobody there now. Whenever I go there I get lost. Yet the fascination remains, and this I put down to an almost morbid sense of sharing at first hand all that is transitory in my lifetime.

Emotionally, my link with Langley died with the death of my mother at the age of 57, when I was in my second term at Gresham's, which in those days was as remote as the North Pole and not even connected to the telephone. I was brought back twice during her last illness, telephone messages being relayed by the school doctor, and it was during these periods of well-meant enforced idleness that I experienced the more desolate forces of only childhood and home loneliness. The moves cut me off from school and the relationships just started there. At home, the various members of the family who had gathered spoke in hushed voices about the weather and what they had read in the *Daily Mail*. They did not want to hear about school. They would not talk in my presence about my mother. My instinct told me she was dying and my visits to the nursing home left me in no doubt that it would be soon. I accepted this. She died in me before she died, in fact. There was nobody I could talk to about this. These grown-ups would never talk about death. The house, the bow-fronted cottage we had moved to after the war, became alien. When at last they brought my mother's body home to lie in the dining-room, with the bow-window curtains drawn and the door locked, I was asked if I wished to see her and I refused. I was dry-eyed at the funeral and overheard them talking about 'a brave little boy'. When they started the funeral tea, I slipped away up the road to the tree called Canada and was pissing on it when they found me. They welcomed me with embarrassed endearments and found me strange. I was. I was a stranger.

Everything that was feminine, maternal, deep-loving,

breast-warm, everything that was woman, had gone out of my life. Being an only child made this crisis of grief more acute, yet I believe that it also gave me some additional edge of strength. There is an almost violent self-sufficiency which only children can develop. I went upstairs and took a glove of my mother's. I carried it in my trouser pocket for a few days. Before I was sent back to school, I buried it in an uncultivated part of the garden. I offered up a prayer, very cool, very non-committal. It was a moment of wonder, of cake, of self-knowledge. I was immature. I was grown-up. I carried no other souvenir or photograph of her. All my life, I was to seek her likeness in others.

This was hard on my father. He had never established much communication with me. Now we had a few years thrown together with the little Langley house frozen into inertia. Nothing was changed, though everything declined. An ancient daily woman came in. With the family of Uncle George, there were card games several evenings a week. Nobody under the age of thirty, and certainly no likely ladies, entered the front room where the chintz, so proudly made up by my mother, faded into lifelessness. Since then, I have never cared for chintz. My father's routines of filling the time till bedtime (ten o'clock), included a little spaced-out shopping by bicycle and the less strenuous side of gardening. He got the meals himself. They tended to be labour-saving too. It did not seem to matter to him too much whether I was there or not. It was not a home to which I could bring people. It was a relief, I think, when I left and became an occasional weekender.

Because farming was in a bad way, he was relieved also that I had not followed family tradition and taken to the land. He had remarked often that however bad things were on the farm, the auctioneers still prospered. He was very content that I went straight into the respected firm of auctioneers and estate agents, Hillier Parker May & Rowden, though they did not touch livestock or agricultural land. In fact it was a very sophisticated business, concentrating on commercial property and investment. I was there because Mr and Mrs Hillier, themselves childless, lived in what had once been called the newer part of Langley. There was a hint that one day I might make good. Meanwhile, as I struggled at the bottom, Mrs Hillier gave me an evening meal one day a week and loaded me with kindness which included advances for my first motorbikes. I loved big, comfortable Mrs Hillier, whose husband called her Jumbo. When I did anything at all creditable, like having a poem in print, she would always say how proud my mother would have been. Nobody else spoke of my mother.

When I took up my quarters in Soho, Mrs Hillier was dismayed as if I had gone to live in a foreign country. She was reassured when I explained that my place was just behind Liberty's. She lived surrounded by the pastel shades of Liberty's.

Soho has changed less in my lifetime than any district in London. The clubs and pubs change hands. New generations of market people, shopkeepers, film handlers and dealers in human flesh crop up and look like their predecessors. I was happy in the place, rent collecting and dealing in a very junior way with the letting, selling and buying of property. Considering I had never set foot in any city other than Canterbury, my adoption of London was amazingly sudden and quick. Professionally, it was my job to know it; what trade went with what district, not just fish at Billingsgate but also the rag trade north of Oxford Street; what were good or bad residential and shopping areas and, above all, what was promising as development potential. This was not an aesthetic but a political education. London was owned by people.

Freeholders were incredibly powerful. Some were Dukes, some were institutions, some were speculators, some came to the office to buy up parcels of slum property for 'improvement', after 'getting the people out'. The invisible, often well-concealed pattern of ownership, of power behind the facades of my adopted city turned my adherence to the romantic Left, with its symbols of tractors and pylons, into more radical lines of thought.

By the time I had passed all my qualifying exams and was ready for promotion I found myself repelled by the whole business. It provided a service, certainly, but it was geared to make nothing but money. The dealers, speculators, developers and exploiters were the moving forces. Profits were not made by manufacture or production, but by the often unsavoury skills of people who manipulated those who manufactured or produced. I was not going to devote the rest of my life to this sort of job. I was careful not to talk high-mindedly about this. Many good and respected friends accepted the profession without question. I had already learned to respect a man for what he is, not for what he does. I slipped away without fuss, with smiles all round, my political convictions deepened but muted. Only childhood is good training for that sort of thing.

Mr Hillier had stood as a Liberal candidate in the early thirties, which had scandalised the tennis party society of Langley. I wondered if I could talk to him of the doubts that had caused me to leave his firm and the prospects, distant though they were, of succession to the top. But he cut across all that by congratulating me in good old Liberal style on 'bettering' myself. There was no room for artistic temperament in the business, he added wistfully, for he loved to sing romantic ballads accompanied with Amazonian emphasis by the Vicar's daughter at the piano.

The change of profession from real estate to broadcasting

was too much for my father. "He goes and qualifies as a surveyor then turns himself into an engineer," he complained to cronies in Slough market.

"I'm not an engineer," I told him. "I'm a sort of writer-producer."

"If you're in the BBC, you must be an engineer." He countered, "When the set goes wrong it's an engineering job. The headquarters must be full of engineers."

"But I'm *writing*."

"That's not work. People aren't going to pay you good money to do that."

Though we remained on most amicable terms, I never quite convinced him that I had not become, mystifyingly, an engineer. When the Second World War came and I first appeared as a RAF officer, he knew he had been right all along. "You can't be in the Air Force without being an engineer." When the stripes on my sleeve thickened, his conviction was confirmed. "Funny that he should end up as an engineer," he said, just before he died in 1944.

In the mid-thirties it was not fashionable to be in the BBC. Members of the intelligentsia assumed a pitying attitude with murmurs of 'wasting your talents'. It was not a literary occupation. It was a form of creative prostitution. Even T. S. Eliot, always kind and shrewd in his advice, was a little patronising toward the new medium. "There are some young fellows in the BBC, who are interested in what they call radio drama," he had written to me. "They have got hold of poets and teach them what they need to know about the technique. It might be worth while seeing them while the fit is still on them." When the war came, the BBC became a reserved occupation, much favoured by the intelligentsia, a fashionable alternative to uniform.

After the rough and tumble of the property world, the BBC

seemed to me incredibly gentlemanly, a well-mannered world with news readers in dinner jackets and the formidable Reith reigning aloft and aloof. It was rather stylish, though many of us were overworked and underpaid. Part of the atmosphere hinted that it was a privilege to be there at all, no matter what the intelligentsia, politicians and members of the Establishment might think.

I had moved out of Soho into Charlotte Street, where the famous Fitzroy was my local and the legends of Fitzrovia, now the subject of serious documentaries, were no taller than the bar stools, and you could cash a cheque for £1 which was as much as one dared the bank with. But soon my heart took off from Charlotte Street to Hammersmith to Crystal Herbert. Their tall house, with the reflection of water on the ceilings, the throb of tugboat engines and the noises of water fowl in the early mornings, became a second home bringing me back to the Thames, playmate of my boyhood at Langley, and boast that my father had once farmed at Runnymede.

When we married, we lived at first on the river front at Richmond. During my BBC years, we had a converted lifeboat, with a diabolically moody motor-car engine, which cut out whenever we approached a bridge, resulting in our shooting many bridges sideways on. But we moved up and down river in the summer, taking weekly seasons to Broadcasting House.

My leaving the BBC after five years was one of the few really wise decisions of my life. I joined the *News Chronicle* as a columnist, which from every point of view, except that I doubled my money, was one of the more foolish acts of my twenties. The BBC had taught me the techniques of a then new medium and, more importantly, had sent me to work in the north of England. There in Salford, Jarrow, Leeds I met unemployed industrial workers. I went down coal-mines, into shipyards and mills, and discovered some of the realities which had been lost to me in the south where they made nothing except money. I was grateful for this industrial experience, belated and superficial though it was. But, back in Broadcasting House, intuitive warning lights told me that this was all too pleasant, too softly demanding for the creative writer which I hoped I might be. It was a job for life. In those days there was no alternative unless one went abroad. It seemed it was unheard of for roving programme staff to resign. Did I realise I was losing a pension? Did I realise that there was no way back? Did I realise that it wasn't done to walk out of a safe job so full of promise for a man with a young family?

One of the most dangerous and debilitating notions of matrimony, then and now, is *settling down*. The husband is supposed to start working toward a pension, seeking security and respectability, while the wife has a family and gives up a professional career for part-time work. Pleasure depends on the availability of sitters in. Adventure goes out of life, to reappear shockingly when the kids become teenagers and start hitch-hiking to Amsterdam or Katmandu. Crystal and I managed to avoid those marriage clichés which were urged on us by those who knew 'what was best'. She encouraged me to jump the safety of the BBC for the hazards of Fleet Street. Even though she was nursing our second child, she enthusiastically supported our move to the country, to a comely farmhouse between Dunmow and Thaxted in the East Anglia of my forebears, and in the most impractical location for anyone writing a daily column on a national newspaper.

I was acting out my yeoman role—with all the odds against me—and indulging an obsession for places whilst proclaiming then, as now, that I can work anywhere, and that a writer should be indifferent to surroundings. All that had been eroded from Langley was here in natural seemly order and abundance at Tilty Hill. A dairy herd at our back door. Fields of arable land beneath the front windows. Threshing in the yard. Shooting for the pot. Our own donkey which stole candles—there was no electricity. In the village and round about were self-respecting country folk with whom we were at once at ease. While part of me laboriously travelled into Fleet Street every day and thence on to a columnist's hectic round, with good expenses, much free entertainment and all too regular booze, the would-be yeoman lived up the simple country life—in snatches. It was hard work but it was good fun, and I often wonder how long it would have gone on and whether it would have given us all happier lives if the war had not intervened. We clung on to Tilty Hill while I was in the service but petrol rationing and education problems beat us. No sooner had I written a book *The Green Grass Grew All Round*, celebrating the place and not mentioning war, than we moved off to the Westerham Valley which was more accessible, though it immediately became a target area for flying bombs and rockets.

At Tilty Hill, we had dug trenches in the orchard during the last days of peace. When war was declared, I was no longer there but back on my cherished Thames. The village postmaster, limping from his First World War wounds, delivered a telegram with a good deal of ceremony and his accustomed air of one who knew all the answers. "This is it, Mr P.," he said gleefully, and to underline his statement, a balloon, adrift from the London barrage, came sailing over. He gazed at it and added portentously, "Seems as if they're using gas again this time."

The horror of this idiotic remark was dramatised for us by one of the RAF fighters from Debden, which tore about playing the balloon for a few moments, like a toreador, before shooting it down. This, we decided, signalled the end of civilisation. I possessed no war equipment of any kind. I packed espadrilles and a *blouse marine*, snatched up my civilian gas mask and set out for London, giving the postmaster a lift as far as the village, where he eagerly told the world that I had joined the Navy.

This was far from the truth. Though for some reason it was an Admiralty signal that summoned me to the colours, I went to join a most unwarlike vessel, newly painted white and Oxford blue, APH's *Water Gipsy* at her 'appointed station' at Lambeth Pier. During the last of the peace, our family had spent many happy hours aboard her during a cruise from Hammersmith to Oxford. Now she was embodied in a somewhat nebulous organisation, the River Emergency Service, as yet only remotely controlled by the Royal Navy. A reassuring professional touch was provided by a sedate sea scout, in a smart badge-bright uniform, who knew absolutely everything about nautical matters. I never knew how he came to join us, or by what high authority he was sent. I am ashamed to admit that if I even knew his name, I have now forgotten it. I suspect that he was destined to great things. Everything about his grave demeanour suggested this. He possessed a whistle on a lanyard, a jack-knife in his stockings and a diary. It was the diary which grew to be formidable. Early on, we observed that he was logging not only the movements of the ship, but the comings and goings of ourselves—at least we had that impression. He was calm almost to the point of austerity. His manner was polite but objective. If I got myself tied into knots, he rescued me without a trace of contempt. He always knew where to find the skipper's peaked cap.

On the day war broke out we anchored off Westminster Steps in order that APH, who was at that time a Member and one of our rulers, should attend the House at such a momentous time. Members waved to us from the Terrace as we put him ashore. Our presence, combined with the balloon barrage, must have given some military reassurance.

As we waited for our Captain to return and war to be declared, I recollect looking at Westminster Bridge with something of the intentness of William Wordsworth looking away from it. Buses and trams were going over peacefully enough, but there were already signs of the times. There were, for instance, three men urging an elephant across towards the South Bank. This surely was an evil omen. I glanced at the sea scout, who was busy with his fountain pen. Was he noting the beginning of a national panic?

Such were my last thoughts before war was declared. The family portable, among the ashtrays on the table in the forward cabin, gave us Chamberlain's declaration. The sea scout got most of it down. Then, as everyone knows, the sirens went off. Our first instinct, having salt water in our blood, was to get steam up, which we did by cranking the engines. We told ourselves that we should at least be in motion when the end came. But in the next breath we all told each other that we could not possibly move without our Captain.

Misty-eyed with panic, some of us searched for the handle of the winch which would heave up the anchor, while one of us put off in the pram dinghy to the steps beneath the Terrace of the House. APH, with a characteristic sense of duty, came out of the House at the double. Simultaneously, crowds of MPs came out on the Terrace to watch the destruction of the capital. Being the only unit of His Majesty's Services in sight, we were the focus of their whole attention. They cheered—as MPs will—at the sight of the gallant Senior Burgess of Oxford University being frantically rowed towards his command in the pram dinghy. With much fumbling, the tender was secured and the Captain assumed command at the wheel.

Nobody was wearing any headgear so salutes were dispensed with. It was only a matter of minutes before the river-bed and the slimy water disgorged *Water Gipsy*'s anchor, and we moved full steam ahead along the whole frontage of the Houses of Parliament with triumphant dexterity, encouraged by the acclamation of the Members on the Terrace, amazed as we were that such a manoeuvre could be carried out without hindrance from the enemy.

When the all-clear sounded and the anticlimax came, we had reached Lambeth and were doubling back. The MPs had dispersed. The streets were empty. We thought about our homes and families and were quite glad to be alive. Nevertheless, we were all, except for the sea scout, morally and physically shaken by our call to action stations. In the long lull that followed, I glanced over the shoulder of the stern youth; he was writing in a firm hand that war had been declared and that the first raid had been ineffective.

Somebody murmured, "We may as well have our first drink of the war, even if it turns out to be our last."

There was still a degree of choice left over from the days of peace; and we duly chose. But what of the sea scout, writing it all down in his diary with the steadiest hand you ever saw? He must have some reward before any of us raised a comforting tipple to our own lips. What would he have? Without a moment's hesitation he told us. He had noticed that we carried lime-juice. He would have that, he said, with a splash of soda.

Eager hands reached for the bottle of lime near the paint. How much? Was that enough? He liked a good measure. We sploshed in the soda. One day, if any of us survived, we should see this boy drinking rum. Meanwhile, with one accord we raised our glasses. Being a well-mannered youth, he raised his. Being also cautious, he sniffed before tasting.

His clear-cut features crumpled. He flinched. Somebody said encouragingly, "Drink up, me boy! That stuff won't do you any harm."

"Excuse me, but I think it will, sir. It smells like varnish." He sipped. "It tastes like varnish . . ."

It was varnish, of course. Varnish and soda. The varnish that belonged to happier days when artists came aboard not as belligerents, but to paint the sweet Thames.

"I'm afraid I can't drink this stuff, sir, even if there is a war on," said the youth, heaving the tipple over the side and returning to write a further entry in the log. What did he write? If his mature eye should ever fall upon this page, I would stand him a man's drink to know.

The Square Peg

It was fun for the first twenty-four hours. Then it became evident that I was starting the war on the wrong foot—in this agreeable vacuum of amateurish endeavour with Magnus Pyke as a scholarly mate and Victor Passmore the painter sharing the washing-up with me. We were not in the Navy, nor were we civilians. APH was to receive his Petty Officer's Uniform, pay and a White Ensign many months later. I fled, filled in time with the *News Chronicle* as a war reporter having lost my columnist job, and with the BBC running a weekly programme called *Parish Mag*, until I was taken by the RAF.

During my first year, I served as an Intelligence Officer with various squadrons and on various airfields in the west of England. For the rest of the time I was on the move, and at the end of it all reckoned that I had been in forty-five countries during my RAF stint. This was not exceptional and possibly not strictly accurate, but it meant that the best part of family life passed me by, though we had a third child during the war years.

I have no wish now to recall or write about the war. I can only remember episodes and have to search my diaries to see if they existed or if there are bits of personal embroidery. Fear, boredom, separation, loss, humiliation, and also love, happiness and slapstick came and went. I have not the skill or inclination to work back over it all. In my later life I have taken to constructive amnesia, deliberately de-memorising events and people that went with them. This is not quite the same as forgetting. It is rather clearing the past into a limbo nearly out of mind, in order to leave more room and capacity for the present.

I was a square peg in a square hole, a very rough fit sometimes, driven in too hard sometimes. Intelligence duties continued, and special jobs of confidential reporting, but the main commitment was writing articles, pamphlets, or books. These were published anonymously, under offical imprint, or handled by the Ministry of Information credited with a *nom de guerre*. It was a brief, not wholly unsuccessful, essay in State Authorship. It was acceptable only in that one was never compelled to write an untruth or anything which went against one's conscience. Politics did not come into it. The writers who came and went in the Air Ministry unit, nicknamed writer command, were diverse in outlook and talent. The only lasting works which came out of it were the stories written by H. E. Bates, under the pseudonym Flying Officer X. My poetry did not come into it, and it is irksome to find it labelled and dismissed by a younger generation of historians. Robert Hewison, for instance, born in 1943, writes: "The RAF Public Relations Branch ... recognised the usefulness of the poet, John Pudney, whose semi-official poetry earned him comparison (almost certainly unwelcome to the poet) with Rupert Brooke and W. H. Henley."*

I do not recollect ever being compared with these unfashionable heroes, but it may have happened when my back was turned. My only claim is that my poems were spontaneous, never composed at the behest of the authorities. Collectively, they sold a quarter of a million. That was because of the temper of the times. Many of them were

* *Under Siege*: Literary Life in London, 1939/45 (Weidenfeld & Nicolson, 1977)

ephemeral. The one that wears best is *For Johnny*. When it was reprinted in book form in 1975, I traced a little of its history.

It was first written on the back of an envelope in London during an air raid alert in 1941. I was, I imagine, on forty-eight hours leave from RAF Coastal Command Station at St Eval, Cornwall, where I was at that time an Intelligence Officer. There, and earlier on Fighter Stations during the Battle of Britain, I had come face to face with the deaths of men younger than myself—to have just turned thirty was to be a very old man among the squadrons. Some of these losses were very close. Bitterly sudden too, between lunch and tea, half way through an argument or a game, in the midst of lovely country and, in those years, in the domestic setting of England. The experience was repeated far and wide overseas.

There never was a particular Johnny. The twelve lines which forced themselves on me virtually intact in one go, were meant for them all. It is the same with the named individuals in other poems: the one stands for many. Just as men went through a sort of de-identification before taking-off on operations—even required by security to empty their pockets of all personalia—so my verses sometimes re-identified mere numbers as familiar names. To this day, readers continue to identify Johnny and the others with their dear ones, loved ones, acquaintances, comrades or boon companions. This is fair enough. A significant part of the nature of poetry is identification and participation.

As I had worked for the *News Chronicle*, I sent a typescript of *For Johnny*, which the newspaper published. It was signed JP, because it was considered at the time that a serving officer writing under his own name on a 'Service matter'—and surely Johnny was that—would be a breach of regulations.

A pleasant result of its publication was a letter from C. J.

Greenwood of The Bodley Head, saying that he assumed the poem was my work and he would be willing to publish a volume containing this and others. "Just send a selection and I'm sure we shall go right ahead." There were others. And in 1942, a volume called *Dispersal Point* was published, and was reprinted.

Soon after publication, Stephen Potter, then in his pregamesmanship days, devised a BBC programme of *For Johnny* and the other poems with Laurence Olivier, then a naval officer, as principal speaker. Rehearsal and transmission took place during an alert, but that was not the only crisis. The final line of *Combat Report*, a sort of reportage ballad, went: *That's how the poor sod died.*

A warning came somewhere high up that the BBC, even in the throes of war, would not permit the word *sod*. What about *soul*? Make it 'how the poor soul died'? There was a walkout and, while the bombs crumpled somewhere in Greater London, the first broadcast of *Johnny* hung in the balance of an Oxford Street studio.

Eventually, arguments based on poetic licence won and Olivier duly recited *Johnny*; and for the first time used the word sod on the hitherto untainted air of the BBC.

I left *Johnny* in its slim volume, wrote some more, and was sent on duty to Africa, the Middle East, Malta, North and South America and eventually into Europe. I was asked to broadcast the poem in New York and in Cairo, and that seemed to me the last I should hear of it and its companions.

Then came the making of the film *The Way to the Stars*, directed by Anthony Asquith, scripted by Terence Rattigan. A request for the use of *For Johnny* and *Missing* came through the film division of Air Ministry, and I was given some leave to visit the Shepherds Bush studios with the idea that I might help with the presentation of the poems. Here I did little except to salute extras dressed up as Group Captains, and to suggest, without modesty, that *For Johnny* should be spoken *twice*—a reprise being at the end of the film so that the customers took it home, so to speak. It was a contractual curiosity in that the company bought the film rights in the two poems—the first time, we all thought, that the film rights in poems had been an issue.

The poems were spoken by Michael Redgrave and by John Mills; and through their talents reached, and from time to time continue to reach in revival, a public not normally tolerant of contemporary verse.

For Johnny lived on into my middle age with some persistence. Strangers quote it at me at unexpected moments—a commissionaire opening a door, a garage receptionist with tears in her eyes, a North Sea trawlerman, a girl in the Embassy at Athens. A truck driver said he and his wife recited it together 'to feel cosy'. It appeared without my knowledge in *The Oxford Dictionary of Quotations*. It has been used three times on gravestones. The last six lines of it were found on the body of a burnt pilot—could I supply the first half? Raymond Blackburn quoted it in the House of Commons in a debate on Housing.

I feel proud, humble and battered in turn; for it all belongs to another life, a generation ago and too many well-meaning people expect one to go on writing the same thing over and over again for the rest of one's time

My poetic life has been a football match. The war poems were in the first half. Then an interval of ten years. Then another go of poetry from 1967 to the present time of writing. The second half, for better or worse, is for me unconcerned and unaligned with the first.

Though the RAF did not dabble in poetry, it did nothing to discourage the stuff. Coming from civilian life with its preconceptions about the hard-bitten down-to-earth character of a wholly mechanised junior service, it was surprising to find an inherent liberalism toward the arts in the RAF. It broke out in unexpected places. Sir Richard Peck, Deputy Chief of Air Staff, was a brilliant fast-talking little man, who made you sit in a chair and hold tight while he tore about the room footballing ideas. I had mentioned that Benjamin Britten had just returned from the USA to face the war in this country. Benjamin had been in touch with me already and said that he meant to be a conscientious objector; he had asked me about non-combatant work.

"Stop that for goodness sake," Peck said. "Can you find him at once?"

"Yes, a work of his is being performed at the Albert Hall this evening."

"Go along and offer him the RAF Orchestra."

At the Albert Hall, I asked Benjamin if the idea of an orchestra appealed to him—feeling a little out of my depth. He did not take me quite seriously. He was always good-humoured, but this was a very critical time for him—having made the hazardous crossing of the Atlantic, for what?—and he thought I was trying to be funny. I explained at once that it was the RAF Orchestra and that I spoke with the authority of the Deputy Chief of Air Staff. For a moment it was wonderful. Then Benjamin asked if he would have to wear uniform. "You couldn't very well not," I told him, "but I'll have a try."

It was of course hopeless. Peck said, "Pity. Couldn't have a chap doing it in tails."

When I lined up at the end of the war at the demobilisation centre for free issue of civilian clothes off the ration, I was classified as size Portly. I was in my mid-thirties and I was putting on weight.

Of course it should have been a time for taking a sabbatical away from oneself, or what, in after years, we called dropping out. In the thirties, when I had been fretting about participation in politics and how to go on being a writer, T. S. Eliot wrote: "I know, having to think about politics, etc. does get in one's way badly. The only way to get anything done nowadays is to take a period of time and refuse to think about anything extraneous till it is over. Or else get yourself into a position that the thing *has* to be written or you will get into difficulties with other people."

There was no time to take heed of this in the thirties. Everything was peremptorily settled by war. One went on thinking politically, and writing poetry and prose, and loving; but the uniform had the first say, deciding the where, when and how of everyday life. In the forties, when it was all over, the need was to take time and think. No doubt some better integrated people did so. For me, the pressures were immediate and diverse. I went to meet them with a new image.

I took my age and size very seriously. The yeoman image had gone. In its place was a more sophisticated role. Portly indeed; a middle-aged man of the world, a professional writer with a foot in politics, with country roots and urban appetites, very much a *paterfamilias*, doing the best for the children, but also doing himself well, a bottle of wine on the table at lunch and dinner, aperitifs over the road at the snug pub—"I'm just going across to get a box of matches."

Where was love? Where was quality? Where was God, some deeper faith not just an Old Man in the Sky? Or, indeed, in hindsight I would add, where were disillusion, disenchantment, protest? These I think were swilled away with a good deal of enjoyment and bonhomie.

Easy enough to accept that the portly person was reacting naturally to a social mood which said, "now it's all over, let's get down to some real living, make up for lost time, make fun and money". That sort of acquisitive euphoria existed—as a mood. The portly image went along with it and was happy. Yes, I was happy, most of the time. Just as one can be unhappy, indeed despondent doing the right things, one can be happy when things are going, and have gone, wrong. I did not give myself time to think about values, question happiness, or notice that acquisitiveness and quantity could mean loss of quality. When the moments of wonder, of innocence broke through I rejected the cake, hastily shrouding it, and laughed it off in an alcoholic haze. Only a haze, mark you, not a debauch. Portly meant dignified. Cake also symbolises an aspect of love which is wonder. Was love a casualty of war and of post-war euphoria?

If you had asked me at that time when I was taking my age and size so seriously, I should have taken you up and talked of love as a man of the world. It was not till later, after I had run out of happiness, when the portly gent had faded, and no poetry had beckoned me with wonder, that I realised that I knew nothing of love and nothing about poetry. This was not a sudden flash, a hectic conversion; rather, it was a slow revelation on the road to Emmaus. It required a new humility which had nothing to do with hymnal Lamb of God clichés, but was almost aggressive in its self-awareness. I was not better because of my age and experience. Certainly I had no edge over others. I do not believe in the older-and-wiser myth. I saw love in the terms of wonder and mystery. Poetry beckoned to me again. I was not just seeking the image of my mother and coping with preconceived notions and barely-bridled lusts.

Loving

When my mother died, during my fourteenth year, I was deprived of femininity. There were two little girls living next door who were much too young. At Canterbury, where I spent holidays with my father's family, there were two aunts for ever proclaiming brightly, "We're not as young as we were." Gresham's School at this time was bereft even of talk of women. There was some physical dalliance, painfully furtive, not with incipient homosexuals but with individuals who were to start large families a few years later. This was sex as a sport. It was separate from intimate friendships, from love, from tenderness. This attitude was not simply a result of boarding-school, a dormitory product. I have since noticed it in people educated at day-school, even at co-educational schools.

It was the attitude that I carried into adult working life, where at the office and at the football club sex talk proliferated, constantly spiced with dirty stories, the liturgy of anti-love. It was all very normal: sex was a sport until love intervened, and then you went steady until you atrophied or became a dirty old man—the English euphemism for a satyr. Deprived of femininity and tenderness, which I still associated with my mother, without confidants or even intimate friends at hand, very wary inside myself, outwardly light-hearted, I stepped out of boyhood into the fringes of manhood. I blame no one for these attitudes. My father and his family were constitutionally incapable of endearment. I never heard the word darling in domestic or social use. That was the way they were made. But I didn't feel deprived. I went stumbling and sprawling into the territories of love. No doubt I looked coltish and that attracted some people. I pursued and was pursued. It was a promiscuity not so much of lust as of curiosity driving me toward that essential innocence which is the beginning of the knowledge of one's own nature, the realisation of tenderness, of respect, of not hurting.

I was beautifully mixed-up at this time, when the air would smell of apricots while I wrote soft-centred and forgettable poems about love; I ranged through the office juniors, the season-ticket girls on the GWR, some strictly amateur ladies in Soho and passing goddesses encountered socially in the wealthier climate of the Hilliers. Diana—she has to be called that—was one. She rode a rather heavy horse round two very green fields, rarely elsewhere, taking a few easy jumps. She began pink and white and became gloriously puce and hot. She was totally given over to horsemanship. "If you could only ride, John. Mummy might let you have the other horse," were the words she used which I took to be a challenge.

In those days in the Home Counties, equestrianship hovered on the fringes of wealth, and even to get a quotation for a riding lesson took several days. My father, who had hunted incessantly in his younger days before he put that—among all other activity—behind him, said, "That's all very well, but what are you going to *wear*?" I roamed the cast-off clothes shops of Praed Street, Paddington, where taxi-drivers in those days bought huge ankle-length overcoats, and found a pair of yellow riding boots with spurs thrown in. These took my fancy as romantic and were a token of my intention of saving up for a couple of riding lessons. The following weekend I wore them to ride my motor-bike to report to Diana in their Tudor-style manor house (now a public library) overlooking the two green fields (now an adventure playground). The equestrian scene was deserted. "She fell off again just after you were here," her mother told me. "Her heart was really in ballet. She's taken it up with all her usual keenness. She won't be back till quite late. What fancy boots you've got, John ... and spurs on a motor-bike!"

I was bruised by this, but the air still smelled of apricots as I drove out through the wrought-iron gates. Bruises were to be expected. I sighed for Diana for the last time as I pulled up at a telephone-box, rang Pauline, and persuaded her to come to a Palais de Danse and, glaring at my footwear, would she bring a pair of her brother's shoes.

I recall such idylls now not to suggest any special potency on my part, but to detect the note of bewilderment and dismay which went with them. Why did they start so fair, and finish, with or without bruises, and usually of my choosing, so soon? I was susceptible to every kind of attraction; and when there was failure, there usually had to be compensation—me putting it right with myself, a typical, and useful only-child routine.

This teenage motor-cycle-mounted Don Juan phase had many bizarre moments. There was the Saturday evening when one of the wing three-quarters and I began an affair in the shower, which went on to mutual seduction aided by a bottle of Cointreau at his flat. When he suggested bed I declared, smiling but austere, that I always slept in my own, accepted a mug of black coffee and, with the aid of the night air forced into me on the old Great West Road, returned to my perch in Soho. I felt good and then I wondered if I should feel good. Suppose I got stuck like that? The childhood threat 'if you make a face you get stuck like that'. The logical, though expensive move was to go toward Piccadilly and pick up what we then used to call 'a bit of fluff'. But our neighbour in the back room, now out on her own beat, had made me swear over early morning teas with buttered toast never to resort to street-walkers. "You'll manage on your own, John. No need for you to buy anything. Keep it like that, boy, promise?" So I sallied forth, still heading for Piccadilly, goaded only by the resolution to prove myself to myself.

At that time, I had never been inside a big hotel. This surely was the time for breaking new ground. So I entered the Regent Palace Hotel and drifted about the foyer, savouring its glamour. It must have been my apparent innocence which saved me from being thrown out. It was reckless arrogance which beamed me on to a girl at the enquiry counter, who tried to stifle a yawn as she watched me approaching. "Are you tired?" I said.

"I expect you would be if you'd been working as long as I have. Looking for someone?"

"You!"

I must have said it with some passion because she, Margery, with her damson-coloured hair, met me at the staff entrance twenty minutes later, looking wide-awake. Mockingly, she counted the stairs up to my room. "Didn't I tell you I was tired?"

I forgot the bit about proving myself to myself. It was a new sort of attachment, another aspect of love. For Margery had been hurt by a teenage runaway marriage. She wanted no ties. She wanted to go on with her job. She wanted a companionship of love. I couldn't believe it when she said, "Let's go on seeing each other now and then." But she taught me a new dimension of love, which was mutual respect. After some months of 'now and then', she told me dispassionately that she was going back to the north of England to marry a cousin, a little older than herself, who was in the catering trade, had been waiting for her and wanted to start a family. She thanked me for 'coming in out of the night'. My gratitude to her has grown with the years. She taught me that promiscuity was not a way of life; and that I should not always be looking for the image of my mother. I did not give up the sport. I just recognised it for what it was.

The Don Juan on a motor-bike image was more or less drowned in the English Channel. Though my mother had travelled to and from Australia several times, and my parents had daringly taken their honeymoon in Switzerland, they regarded Europe as a Dark Continent with frightful language and food hazards. So I had grown up without a whiff of abroad—an unimaginable situation to my children and grandchildren. Hitching was unknown but hiking was coming in. Germany had started youth hostels. With a smile of defiance at the generation which went on saying 'the only good German is a dead one', I went to Cologne with a rucksack and two companions from the office. In Bonn, we tangled with four young Germans and travelled up the Rhine and along the Moselle with them, being embodied in the *Wandervogel*.

With three of these four I formed an attachment which was of instant emotional intensity. It was based on curiosity at first, then it shifted to the sharing of ideas as we shared each day's journey. For them this was *brudershaft*. For me it was mysterious, sentimental, tender, affectionate, idealistic, platonic (as interpreted to me years later in the letters of Marcello Ficini). It was not sexual with those three. The fourth, Hans, was in fact homosexual and kept himself at a distance, though nobody was censorious and took in good part his advances which were sometimes heavy.

That year we saw Hitler. It was a wet evening and he and the audience seemed to be steaming. He wore his raincoat like a straitjacket. His hands were pudgy. Jochen tried to translate in a whisper but had to give up when people scowled at us. He and Wilhelm were not impressed. Werner was thoughtful and argumentative. Hans was starry-eyed.

The following year, I stayed at their home town in Saxony. I realised for the first time that the four of them came from quite separate social strata and income groups, their parents hardly knowing one another. I lodged with Jochen, whose father was a senior teacher, and Jochen carried me off now and then to join him in his *luft-bad*, a sun-bathing enclosure used as a club by professional gentlemen. Quite nude, they gravely discussed the affairs of the world, and were unanimous in telling me that Hitler would never get anywhere because it was economically impossible—British pundits were still saying it in the forties when Hitler was in control of Europe.

With Jochen, Werner and Wilhelm the intensity of friendship was renewed. Hans was effusive physically, but unwilling to let things go too deep emotionally. He was demonstrative in horseplay with the girls. These Saxon girls for me were dazzling, uninhibited, always laughing and suddenly falling into serious discussion of some really unlikely subject. They were, of course, enjoying me as a novelty and practising their English. But, at the time, I took it all at its face value. I learned to waltz like a Saxon and soon floated off my feet into the romantic tenderness of an affair with Ilse. The girls did not distract but rather enhanced the intimacy of my *Wandervogel* comrades.

"You love Jochen and he loves you." Ilse explained, as she took me into her arms and we lay hot with dancing the night before I left. "When I come to England I will bring news of him."

Only a bedside table with a wobbly vase of flowers separated Jochen's bed from mine. Every night and morning he would lean across and shake hands formally. On the last morning he said contentedly "Now, you and Ilse will be happy in England, won't you."

This German idyll which had so enriched me was destroyed piece by piece during the thirties. Ilse came to London fleetingly then took a post in a very strict girl's school on the South Coast. There was never anywhere for us to dance in the Saxon manner. She rode on my pillion and on Sunday afternoons when she was free we lay on the downs, watched the clouds and read the latest letter from Jochen. Soon, though, she was crying to go back. The clouds over Saxony were of a darker hue.

I saw Werner in Munich briefly after that. From him, and from the letters of Jochen and Ilse when she returned and married 'because of the bad times', I had some idea how my idyll fell apart. Werner, whose family owned an engineering works, argued no more but simply shrugged and said it was a business necessity to be in with the Nazis; he hoped it was secretly and not too deeply. Jochen's father had been under direct threat; his livelihood, his pension, Jochen's future as a teacher. They had capitulated and joined the party. Ilse's marriage had been pestered by a fleck of Jewish blood in her veins of which I had never been aware. Her husband was Danish which implied an escape route. The one who had really come into his own was Hans. He had already been promoted within the National Socialist Party. And Wilhelm? Nobody liked to say exactly. He had been denounced by Hans as a homosexual with Jewish blood and left wing views. He had gone to what they called a 'place of education'. That was how it was. Our correspondence dwindled and died.

Compared with the inter-continental travel enjoyed by so many of the young in the seventies, my hectic plunges into Europe, with bits of time off and a few pounds, may be tame enough. Somehow I managed trips to Prague, Warsaw, Berlin and Vienna. I discovered, too, that very few pounds were needed for weekend trips to Paris. This travelling was not just notching up miles, it was a romantic gesture of liberation. I would not be hemmed in by the conformity I had had to accept in a so-called dynamic London office. The motor-bike had been the first self-assertion, Europe was the next; the third, and most important, was love. I didn't give it that label at the time. I was shy of that single all-purpose word which was so much easier to use in German.

Ilse was a few years older than myself. It could have been that, or an actual quest for my mother's image which turned me toward women—'older women' is the nasty expression carelessly bandied about. I mean women in contrast simply with girls. Age labels are stuck on by onlookers and are usually irrelevant. In early youth one is made conscious of a few years difference, but in fact age differences often enhance relationships. Sukey brought up the matter by saying she was old enough to be my aunt. She was just finishing off a divorce. She had two children who must never see us in bed together. She always had her elbows out, washing things, assembling oniony stews; and in a shed near the back door, making pottery which she had a knack of selling to high-class shops. She was tawny, lithe and wonderfully untrammelled by her domesticity. The children laughed a lot, took me for granted and slept all through each night. Sukey and I might have known each other all our lives.

"We are precarious," she said. "You are looking for mother; I am celebrating."

We laughed about this precariously. Then we woke up one morning in the small hours, frightened, and listened to the dawn chorus.

"Put on your clothes and go away, John."

"I want to stay—for keeps."

"Go without looking back. I'm going to Scotland."

She used to tell me she was a moralist and that everything, however outrageous, was good so long as no one got hurt. This, for me, has the true ring of innocence. But at the time I wept, and she went to Scotland that very day. I did not look back but considered myself hurt, and drank a few draughts of self-pity.

I was not so much seeking a mother as being swept away by *panache* when I fell for Ursula, a doctor of medicine, more than a decade older than myself. She was American and had come to London from South Africa to do some course. She had taken a furnished flat on the edge of Regent's Park and possessed a car, a Talbot, which she was all too ready to let me drive. She worked very hard at a kitchen table which she had installed in the elegant drawing-room, but she was determined to make the most of her short stay in this country. So we tripped about the country at weekends. Because she insisted on it, we paid a visit to my father, who was gravely polite but dumbfounded until Ursula, who was married to a cricketer, began to talk about cricket with amazing verve. They then talked cricket for a solid hour. When I next met my father he said, "That was a very intelligent woman. A bit above your head, I would have thought."

Ursula was a vehement dancer. This was good as I have always been, even after sixty, at least a fervent dancer. So one or two nights a week we went dancing. On the really memorable Friday night during our brief affair, she had gone straight to the Palais de Danse from some lecture, carrying a capacious hold-all which went everywhere with her. After an hour or so, we took a taxi to Regent's Park. We were pleasantly tired and it was an amorous ride. We had been indoors for about ten minutes when she cried out, "The skull, the Missing Link!"

She had brought this to England to show to top anthropologists. It was of international importance. It had been discovered by her uncle. She was its custodian. It had to be always kept under lock and key.

"When am I going to be allowed to see it?" I said.

Her voice rose hysterically. "You may never see it. I've left it in the taxi. It's in my hold-all. I promised to take it to University College tomorrow. And now ..." She did not weep. She began to stride about, eyes blazing, cursing herself. "Now we may never see it again. How do you trace a cab in this goddamned country?"

"He'll probably find it and bring it back. Otherwise there's the Lost Property Office. Perhaps it has your name on it?" I suggested fatuously.

"Why should it have my name on it? It's one of the most important anthropological discoveries of the century."

"What about the other things in the hold-all?"

"Just text books and some blank notebooks I bought."

This was years before I had any newspaper contacts. It suddenly struck me though that there could be a headline: MISSING LINK LOST.

"The best thing we can do is to get it into tomorrow's paper. It's quite a story, Ursula."

"The publicity would just about kill my reputation as a doctor and research worker."

"It's more likely to get it back than just sitting here hoping. And the Lost Property Office won't be open till Monday."

So I telephoned the *Daily Mail*, giving both my own name and address and Ursula's, for propriety's sake. It was indeed a story. It went in big on the Saturday morning, and by nightfall Ursula, still besieged by reporters, had the Missing Link. The taxi-driver, quite awed by what had travelled from a Palais de Danse in his cab, received a generous reward and so did I! The *Daily Mail* paid me for the tip off.

The air was sweet again, when I fell in love with Crystal in Hammersmith, in Paris, in Bavaria. We had a white wedding, a Pullman car to Brighton and the bridal suite at the Royal Albion Hotel. It was presided over by Sir Harry Preston, an Edwardian swell who hobnobbed with Great Sportsmen, Cabinet Ministers, the presentable Intelligentsia, Stage People (we didn't say Showbiz in those days and there were no Telly People) and of course Famous Wits. A honeymoon in the bridal suite was his wedding present as a friend of the family. We entered it dazed with drink and awed by the flowers. It was October, and they had the full heating on for our benefit. We spent our last conscious moments prising open the huge windows which would let in the sea air.

In the morning we counted our money and reckoned that we had enough to cover tips and a taxi to the station, with a little over to get us through just one day.

Then came the message that Sir Harry would be delighted to take wine with us at noon. We had nerves, felt the whole hotel was staring at us. "I expect it will be a glass of sherry in his office," I said, "we'll go and fortify ouselves first." We were agreeably launched in a milieu where every social misgiving called for a drink—the Dutch courage talk.

It was an unwise tipple, for the taking of wine with Sir Harry was no cosy corner affair. He had cleared a front lounge overlooking the sea. A table was set with oysters and champagne, and there were three waiters in attendance. It was a feast with extravagant formality. Every drink was a toast. Champagne, according to Sir Harry, was the very essence of life.

"You should ride for an hour first thing, young man. I've had a couple of hours up on the Downs this morning. Then a bottle of the stuff before you sit down to breakfast. Where are you working?"

"I've just started in the BBC."

"Handy for the Park! Take your ride there. Then the Bubbly. Perfect health. You'll never falter. Look at me! We'll drink now to ..."

It seemed that he would never be at a loss for toasts and would never envisage a young couple with our connections being short of a daily bottle of champagne—or a horse. Determined, I suppose to put us through it, he ordered the staff to take an unfinished bottle through to our lunch-table. When we had slept it off, I doled out the expected tips, wrote a note about sudden recall to BBC and fled. We bought coal in paper bags and lived off sardines, until we had the courage to face the Herbert family to explain that we had decided on a working honeymoon after all, and were seeking relief to tide us over. We had five years of peace coming to us.

Within the home, the world was full of promise tangled with success. I wrote my first novel—about Soho—and a string of fantastical short stories in a style seemingly effortless at the time, which I have never been able to pick up again. They adapted well to radio and even to the exigencies of pre-war television. As a columnist, the hard grind was sugared with expenses and much free entertainment. One started the day with a glass of champagne at El Vino's. But, whatever the promise and material success, there was a sense of foreboding very marked, of course, in the Liberal-Left *News Chronicle* where I worked.

Whenever I have written biography, I discover there significant 'turning points' in men's lives. They can be self-controlled or fortuitous, leaving a portentous query for games of hindsight. Suppose I had stayed in real estate, aided by the blessings of the childless Mr Hillier, and acted steady; would I have been able to develop far better quality in my prose and poetry without financial stress? I still have a feeling that being in business or industry can actually help a writer. And then, of course, that fortuitous turning point, the war? Suppose it had not happened when I was thirty, full of promise, but beginning to succumb to the flesh pots? I think I would have gone down in quality as a writer and made more material demands as a human being. The family would not have suffered constant separation and changes of base. I would have had more acquaintances. More friends would have gone out of focus.

So the portly man who took over at the end of the war had had at least the advantage of an involuntary shake-up and the opportunity for new values to emerge—and to submerge.

Versatility Time

Having one foot in politics was not on. Not for me. If I were backed by a trade union or had a directorship, it might have been possible to battle my way toward the House and survive there. The only other basic source of income might have been in political journalism. But I have never been able to write about politics. It is a total inhibition. I did not even compose my own election address for the General Election of 1945. I enjoyed, and still enjoy, the active side of the game. I see now that I wanted to be an amateur. I could not realise that turning the Beveridge Report into the foundations of a Welfare State was a job for professionals not only idealists. Some were making the sacrifices which I could not bring myself to consider. One or two acquaintances, demobilised sergeants and corporals, were simply roughing it on the Member's £1000 a year pay packet.

My radical conviction went back to the 1929 General Strike, my days as a rent collector among the very poor and my first-hand encounters with industry, the distressed areas as a journalist and the personal impact of Nazism and glimpses of right and left conflicts in Europe. Few left-wingers of my generation had travelled outside Europe, except in service or on a job, and the war gave to thousands a first glimpse of the British Empire and the Dominions. I myself had never set eyes on a black man in his home until I landed in West Africa in 1942. Then I saw a little, a very little for native life was out of bounds, in various West African colonies and in Jamaica and Trinidad. Finally, in Malta, I became aware that even for a European colonial people, altogether lower standards were tolerated. My heart was therefore behind the Labour plans for dealing with the Colonial Empire. Any inclination toward conventional sentimentalism about the Dominions was tempered by having served a stint as Intelligence Officer to a Royal Australian Air Force flying boat squadron (Fucking Limey, we just love you) and getting into a fight in Quebec Province on being refused a drink because I was wearing uniform.

A contributory reason for becoming a Parliamentary candidate in 1945, was a frequent jibe from the older generation in the thirties. "If you have such a strong social conscience, why don't you do something practical instead of marching about and sending poets to the war in Spain?" It was a favourite dig that came from A. P. Herbert, himself representing Oxford University and gaining glory as an Independent in the House. In fact, there were few opportunities for even the most ambitious with a National Government in power from 1935 to 1945. When at last a General Election came, it was time for action, even in a spot where Labour's chances were nil. I was accepted as a candidate for Sevenoaks, an oddly diverse scattered Tory stronghold which touched the outer London suburbs on one side and the outskirts of Maidstone on another. Even to get round it all in time was quite a problem. I did parts of it in an open, stripped-down Bentley, driven by a Group Captain in mufti. We frequently got ahead of the loudspeaker car from which Crystal, my wife, was proclaiming my imminent appearance. Because there had been no General Election for over ten years, nobody quite knew the ropes and experienced people were hard to come by.

VERSATILITY TIME

We did discover, just in time, that the candidate must never buy drinks because it might seem to be buying votes. But there was nothing in the rules to prevent him accepting liquor—and it never occurred to me at that time to miss a drink. There was nothing to eat in the pubs and there were few other places of refreshment in my territory. So one was fuelled mainly on beer.

As the election approached and the pace grew hotter, with four or five meetings miles apart in a single evening, one's physical capacity for drink without food caused the same sort of anxiety that must sometimes beset royalty. After rushing through orchard villages on the outskirts of Maidstone, for instance, attempting to keep to the schedule dictated by the political agent, while chairmen kept meetings together pending my arrival in the ordinated places, I found myself visited by the most urgent of human needs while making an impassioned speech on a platform in a corrugated-iron tabernacle. Determined as I was to give full measure in the face of a stolidly hostile audience, I nevertheless was impelled to rush forward my peroration, waving aside interruptions with the promise to answer all questions at the end. When I sat down to whisper my need to the chairman, half a dozen of the opposition were already on their feet, showering questions.

"Better go round the back," whispered the chairman; and aloud he announced, "The candidate has an urgent call to make. I will answer what questions I can while he is away."

Thus dismissed, I hastened out through a side door to the blessed privacy of the back of the building. Relief was blissful—and prolonged. So much so that I reverted to the boyish delight in forming liquid patterns along the dry corrugated-iron. This, I was told afterwards, reverberated like thunder within the tin tabernacle, moving slowly from left to right behind the chairman's table.

Feeling much better, I lit my pipe and returned to find the chairman blushing in his seat and the audience in a strange repression of silence. Had he cowed them or what? Laughter and cheers greeted me as I took the platform to uphold the white lie and show that I had not been running away, declaring, "Well, ladies and gentlemen, that was a most satisfactory call. Now to business."

This was greeted with a renewed uproar which puzzled me for a long time afterwards. Had I converted the meeting? Perhaps, the chairman thought, when I met him weeks later, I had.

When the eve-of-poll meetings came, I was still in good voice and thoroughly stimulated by the action. I had three spaced-out meetings culminating in a rally in Sevenoaks itself. I felt a surge of conviction, self-assurance and vanity—this last being the main fuel for such a political affray. At the last stop before the rally, I really went to town and there was an ovation which drowned the opposition.

"I know a pub on the way into Sevenoaks where I am sure of a double Scotch," I whispered to Crystal.

"Keep that for afterwards," she said.

"Means going back on our tracks. We'll have it now. Just the thing for the rally ..."

I started well but, as I worked up the short emphatic message about the future of Britain, the resonance began to leave my voice, my mouth began to dry out. Effort to finish took the place of resounding conviction. I did well enough. But, I said to myself, they should have heard me just now down the road. When the cheering had died, I allowed myself the suspicion that that one on the road had taken things the wrong way. But I allowed misgiving to be smothered by the supporters, drink in hand, who were saying I was a bit tired and who wouldn't be.

VERSATILITY TIME

I was not elected but the results were considered good enough for me to be put in the way of by-elections. The first time I was short-listed and looked over by a selection committee before being turned down in what headquarters called 'a near thing', I felt myself breaking into a run as I headed for home. Idealism was trailing along somewhere behind and would soon be lost.

I thought of some of my successful friends now in Parliament for the first time, dedicated to the Welfare State, the liberation of colonial people, sanitation in farm cottages; their idealism shaped to a discipline, in some of them a sense of power being fulfilled. I thought of all the meetings at which I had dealt with questions. Not a glimmer of idealism or indeed much community sense ever came up from the floor. Whatever the issue, the query, hostile or friendly, had always been how does it affect *me*? By the time I reached home, I was wearing my disillusionment with a sense of relief. This was a moment to pause and thank goodness for cake! Stick to the idealism, stop being an amateur in politics, stop being a portly figure. If you are a writer, then for pity's sake write and write well, and stick to quality in writing which is what you really want, with some basic poetry perhaps instead of occasional verse.

I smiled the cake away with my man of the world *savoir faire*. I told Crystal I was joining the golf club with an eye to keeping my weight down. We had about half an acre under cultivation and there could have been plenty of weight-reducing labour in that; but we had started having a man in full time with the vague idea of making the garden pay. We were placing our boy in the best preparatory school in the district. We were getting a new Ford through public relations influence. My publisher was offering me a retainer. There was a lot of magazine work. The air was slightly aromatic with cigar smoke. When the next by-election came along and I was to be short-listed I begged off, saying that writing commitments prevented me from standing again for the time being. I talked a good deal about the family coming first and our having three children to educate.

There was much action in these post-war years. My centre of gravity was Fleet Street. I was virtually free-lancing, rarely making ends meet, not just because of the family commitment but because of the style of living. Always haunted by the idleness of my father, I worked obsessively and with increasing lack of discrimination. The mistake, as I see it now, was in the nature of versatility. There is an important difference between the over-zealous professional, the pen-proud hack who says "I can turn my hand to anything", and the technically well-equipped writer whose versatility is disciplined. For some, specialisation comes naturally and profitably enough, but there is always the danger of the subject ruling the pen and the author becoming type-cast. Labels are all too easily acquired—the historical novelist, the sports-writer, the dramatic critic, the essayist (obsolescent), the writer of children's books. The labels help if you take to the one furrow for life. But I believe that most writers need versatility to sharpen faculties and talent, especially in this century which offers the new media of television, radio and film. In my later years, I have preferred to work on more than one book at a time and to break off to do a television or a stint of journalism when such things come my way. I find the attrition rewarding. There are always those who denigrate this as a Jack-of-all trades attitude, but they are either living in the past or rather badly rutted in the present. In other professions, versatility is readily accepted and admired. Had I been at all adept at figures, I would have chosen to be a chartered accountant, a job which can offer great scope to the imagination, much travel and contact with a diversity of people. An accountant I know headed a huge photographic business, left it, and went on to take charge of a vast agricultural empire. He was neither a photographer nor a farmer; he just possessed an accountant's versatility. Where a writer needs to be realistically based in another profession (and a great many do), accountancy should surely be a good pitch—with the help, perhaps, of a little maths.

My own versatility in the forties and fifties lacked discrimination and recognised the discipline only of necessity. When James Agate, famous dramatic critic and book critic of the *Daily Express* died suddenly, I applied on a postcard to the editor, Arthur Christiansen, for the book job. A telephone call the following day said the job was mine and the first piece would appear two days later. As all review copies went to Agate's flat, I was instructed to go out and buy some new books to fill the first column. With two all-night sittings, the job was done; the lucky authors all unaware that I added to their sales even before noticing them. It lasted only a few months, this overpaid job. The catch was the complete freedom of choice I had—only to be asked afterwards "but why choose those?" The bonus was the benefit of Arthur Christiansen's education in the form of notes that dropped from time to time. On several occasions he wrote a thousand words of comment on an eight hundred and fifty-word review I had penned. When I was sacked I was relieved, though I knew I should not get the same money elsewhere. The odd thing was that I did not try. I plunged straight into the next thing that offered, always murmuring about keeping the wolf from the door.

It was during the forties that television began to re-emerge. I had played along with it during its brief pre-war life in the thirties. I was therefore invited to take part in 'the first post-war Guest Night' chaired by A. G. Street in 1946. I have never managed to keep a cuttings book, but it happens that I saved cuttings over several years in the forties. I wrote about this performance in *Illustrated* magazine. As a period piece, I think some of it is worth reprinting. At that time there were only two TV sets in the neighbourhood, and my family went along to the village builder to view the phenomenon. "Make sure your flies are done up," was the parting family advice; so, every time I saw a camera coming at me, I nervously clutched my parts—a term I had to omit in those pre-permissive society days.

Afterwards I wrote up my experience:

'Here's Arthur Street, greeting a lot of old acquaintances after the war ...'
'But where is he supposed to be? In digs?'
'Or on his farm in Wiltshire?'
'In any case, surely we wouldn't all knock as we come in?'
'Wouldn't there be a butler?'
'I tell you I haven't got a butler.'

The speakers are not, as you might imagine, a new crazy gang in rehearsal, but a sober (it is 4.30 pm) and intellectually robust (though I say it myself), group of citizens facing their first post-war television.

What happens to you when you are televised? People have asked me. 'You get very hot', is my first impression. From 4.30 pm when we began our rehearsal, until 9.30 pm when we were signed off by an unheard gramophone record, playing *Auld Lang Syne*, we were very hot, worried, persevering, but not on the whole unhappy.

The gaunt Victorian inside of Alexandra Palace is exhilarating because of the enthusiasm and camaraderie among the smallish BBC staff which operates television. Everyone knows everyone. Everyone makes suggestions. An intelligent pioneering spirit prevails. In the canteen, the director, Maurice Gorham, producers, engineers, casts; and cleaners meet every day in the food queue, and you may meet those of them with a taste for it in the beer queue, which forms from time to time at the 'Dive', a tin chalet with a cherry-tree shaded garden.

In order to appear before you in A. G. Street's Guest Night programme our ordeal, therefore, was a long one, much mitigated by the kindliness, energy and tact of the newly reassembled team of BBC technicians who lack both the stuffiness and cynicism sometimes displayed at Broadcasting House. Most of the performers meet on the BBC's private bus, which leaves from Langham Place to climb 600 feet through north London to Alexandra Palace. On arrival, we are assigned a communal dressing-room with our names on the door. Then we assemble on the set, which is about the size of an average stage in a village hall, and which is opulently got up to look like wherever it is (we are still not sure), where Arthur Street is giving us a party.

If several of our hearts leap at the sight of the whisky upon our host's table, they soon relapse again when we gather behind the tray and see the word DUMMY upon our side of the bottle. Into the hand of each of us is thrust a single foolscap sheet of paper, headed *Guest Night No. 1*. It is a summary and cue sheet of the proceedings. We can have it for rehearsal, but we are reminded that this thirty minutes is to be *without scripts*—though some kindly soul says that one will be hidden among the books in the bookcase... 'and you can stroll across and seem to be looking at a book and see where you are in the show'.

We sweat a little with the anxiety of performing all this,

and filling in the gaps and looking natural and drinking dummy whisky and not falling over something and not drying up. The lights go on and Mary Adams the producer takes us in hand. She is a great producer of microphone interviews. (Will television, I wonder, not kill the sound radio interview stone dead?) She explains how simple it all is. She stimulates discussion until some of us are arguing with perfect acrimony. She takes suggestions.

The dummy bottle goes. We are to have real beer or cider—only there is not enough cider to go round. Anyway we use, let me hasten to reassure you, empty glasses for rehearsals. Barnett Freedman, the artist and myself, lacking the slimness of first youth, find that settee intolerably low for getting up and sitting down gracefully before a possible twenty thousand televiewers. It is immediately raised on our behalf.

After a run through, in which it is clear that the nimble mind of Arthur Street is taxed to the full in memorising how to lead us through such subjects as education, the arts, sport, war experiences, Jugoslavia, and flying in the Far East, we are given the opportunity of going one by one to view our brethren upon the two-control panel screens upon which the producer views us (and chooses the image to be shown to the public). This is rather satisfactory. We think we don't look too bad.

At eight o'clock we go to be made up. Then we're off... The cameraman, seen in a mist of light, beckons me to look as he runs up. Cow-like, I stare into the dark camera eye. (At home, the builder's wife says, 'Look at him, bless him, he's looking straight at you. Wouldn't you like to go nearer to the screen, Mrs Pudney?').

Somehow our deliberations never falter, but they run into unexpected channels (for television really is extempore). We miss that clever bit I had thought of about literature and war, but we have a fascinating impromptu upon men's combinations. Nobody falls over, nobody dries up. We drink real beer. There are too many glasses because when you put one down you can't retrieve it without getting in the way. ('He's had five drinks already,' they say at home, accusatively).

Our brief blaze of glory comes to an end. The twenty-three kilowatts are switched off. We do not know which of the two cameras which peered at us has been 'alive': we have hardly noticed the microphone slung above our heads. We have almost felt at our ease, though some of us wonder how any of the twenty thousand potential audience can have found us amusing. But, there, please do not write and tell me we were not. It will discourage the first humble participants in a great new venture.

I think perhaps I did not shine as a performer as there were few personal appearances after that. Except for vanity, there was no great inducement. The fee was negligible, the potential twenty thousand viewers somewhat nebulous, and the hours waiting about at Alexandra Palace very wearing. I did, however, write three plays which were duly viewed from the village builder's home. Television really had everyone guessing at that time. I was warned by Sidney Bernstein, who more than most people seemed to be in the know (with Granada subsequently to prove it), that to do a play on television was to kill it as a marketable product. It was quite a surprise, therefore, when several film companies showed interest the morning after the production of *Reunion*, and the Rank people snapped it up for £3,500—and from that day to this never produced it. Many publishers regarded the new medium almost with panic. Would it mark the end of books, indeed of the written word? Curiously, the magazines seemed unaware that they would in fact be the first victims. They went on running trivia laced not too strongly with social commentary.

My bundle of yellowing press cuttings shows an almost frantic diversification of my pen in the late forties. Articles in *Punch*, *The Hairdresser's Journal*, *Everybody's*, *The Observer*, *Illustrated*, *John Bull*, *New York Times*. None of the subjects, except for an interview with Nye Bevan, suggests that this was a time with Labour in power from 1945 to 1951, for instance, when the Welfare State was being created at home, and the Indian Empire liquidated, an unparalleled period of social reform. When I started writing pieces about the royal family, then becoming a popular cult, C. J. Greenwood, the publisher of my poems, who had been giving me a retainer to support my serious prose work, issued a stern warning. "No literary reputation will stand that stuff. If you are silly enough to let someone persuade you to do a royal book, you're sunk."

I wish I had heeded him. For, when George VI died, I had several thousand words already written on him for an American magazine. To turn this into a lightning obituary book was not difficult—in fact most rewarding. How I learnt to hate the sight of that volume in after years. If only Greenwood had been more brutal! I had benefited greatly from his past encouragement. Year after year I brought out a novel or a volume of short stories, in spite of the journalistic rat-race. I am not too ashamed about the output, though half the amount with double the quality would have been better. I am only saddened at the way I did not give myself enough to living and to loving.

At last my young family set me off at a gallop into another literary field—stories for children. I have always found this challenging. Directness, a hard story line, no playing down, and a steady flow of letters from readers. Continuity is important; so in each series I kept the same set of characters, no matter how diverse the settings. *Fred and I*, for instance, had a book-length adventure for every day of the week. A reader from Western Australia wrote:

> 'Dear Mr John Pudney,
>   Are you real? You see noone can be realy sure you are. I enjoyed reading your book, friday Adventure. As friday Adventure was published in 1956, I suppose you might be 100 years old. Could you please write back so I know your really Real. I'm 12 this year. I like writing storeys and poetry. Well goodbye till you write to me. I hope your not dead, Sir.
>   from Sara Greenhalgh'

Adults rarely write so flatteringly.

For years I set aside Mondays for writing children's books and I came to look forward to the weekly stint. I contrived to gather an immediate audience to go over chapters as they were written. When my own children went away to school, or grew up, I had to borrow critics for a work in progress. I was always learning. For instance, I once had *Fred and I* on a sinister uninhabited island with some lively action, when the suspension of disbelief snapped. "How could they do all that without having anything to eat?" remonstrated a ten-year-old, backed delightedly by the rest of the audience.

I thanked them and promised to see to it in the following chapter. So, as *Fred and I* and party planned their next moves, I caused them to stumble upon a cache of stores left behind by an ornithologist who had a grumbling appendix and had to leave in a hurry. As my heros planned, they ate cake, veal and ham pie, crisps, sardines, assorted biscuits. I wove a rich assortment of favourite foods into the narrative. I was rather proud of meeting valid criticism so readily. When I stopped reading there was a silence, and then the withering ten-year-old voice. "Yes, but we didn't want to know *what* they ate. That's boring."

The best I ever did for a young reader was for a boy called Joe, living in a suburb of Sydney. He sent me a photograph of himself, posed with a set of the *Fred and I* days of the week books—with just *Wednesday Adventure* missing. That particular book had gone out of print. Could I help to fill the gap?

His letter reached me the day before I left for Australia—I was writing a book about BOAC at the time—and I took my only spare *Wednesday Adventure* along. Two days later I reached Joe's family by telephone on arrival in Sydney, speaking from the somewhat lush hotel suite assigned to me. He was stricken dumb with excitement, disbelief almost, that I was answering his plea in person. The family accepted my invitation to tea and the presentation of the missing volume. Mum and Dad were stiff with shyness, the young sister was stiffer with organdie. Joe himself looked positively starched. I had ordered a splendid cake, but everything was decidedly heavy going until I noticed that fingers were getting sticky and there was a general move toward the bathroom. It was a bathroom ornate by any standards, bristling with taps and shower attachments. It was the ultimate big city wonder—and it was an instant destarcher. The organdie dress wilted, Dad took his jacket off, Mum stepped out of her shoes and Joe gave me ideas for a *Fred and I* story to be set in the outback. *Wednesday Adventure* was a little damp; but it was the book-signing of a lifetime.

Fred and I were faded out many years ago, though letters about them continued to trickle in during the seventies. I still write for children. It is a sweet invigorating discipline.

VERSATILITY TIME

Perhaps it was the more fruitful skill that came out of the happy-go-lucky post-war period. Happy? You can be happy in the first stages of drowning.

The Fifties

On the way back from Australia in the mid-fifties, I was in Calcutta for a short while. I had been taking some off-the-record trips on the pillion of a young Indian journalist's motor-bike, when I was invited by a very agreeable Sahib to lunch at the Turf Club. My host apologised that as it was a race day Indians were allowed in. The country had been liberated but certain things seemed to be changeless. Rather fatuously, I asked him if he had seen the railway station at night. He said, "We're in the aviation business aren't we?" I described the families living in chalked-off squares on the platforms and how I had seen somebody born and somebody die. He sighed. "Yes, there's a lot of poverty about. I suppose some of the refugees never get further than the station."

Toward the end of lunch, he said, "Funny, we saw somebody looking like you careering along on the pillion of a motor-bike. I said to Joe, 'Looks like the writer-fellow!' But of course it couldn't have been. He's got the use of a car."

Through my stint in the RAF, I had acquired some knowledge of and interest in aviation. So I wrote several specially commissioned books. One, for the Ministry, was a short study of the Royal Aircraft Establishment at Farnborough. There, for the first time, I met men who over a coffee would break off an explanation and write a string of symbols on the tablecloth, murmuring, 'it's simpler put this way'. Reducing so much advanced technology to the language of a layman was quite a headache. The bonus was that I came away with material for *The Net*, the novel I told Donald Maclean about.

For the BOAC book, *The Seven Skies*, I had to travel the air routes, sometimes in the company of Captain William Armstrong, a veteran airline pilot who had written a book about his job and who was attached to me as technical adviser. He was my only experience of an airborne back-seat driver. We would be mooning along happily between, say, Bermuda and New York, when Willie would scrutinise the almost blameless sky ahead and snap out in his Captain's voice. "Just put on your safety belt, John. I don't like the look of it." The cabin staff, of course, looked on dumbfounded, hoping that we would not cause panic, but aware that Willie was much too senior and distinguished to be remonstrated with. Worse still, when we were approaching some busy airport such as Miami, he would shake his head fatalistically and declare, "Fifty-fifty chance whether we make it. Modern airports are death traps." We would then laugh bravely, close our eyes and pray.

The sky had remained virtually empty of God until I began flying. My airborne prayers were not just a matter of 'Nearer My God to Thee', they would be particular and urgent. They were expletives screaming for immediate cover. They were more animal than human. They often cried, "Get me out of this," or asked for a good take-off or landing. Since hearing about World War I as a child, I had been burdened by the fear of being afraid. One of my first published poems in the twenties revealed a little of this:

> How will I hold myself,
> How will I keep my stance,
> Now at the frontier of commonsense,
> Now I am faced about
> To meet my chance?

THANK GOODNESS FOR CAKE

> Is it much easier
> To hold on with one's fear,
> To grip a rifle in the frightened air,
> Crouched on the knee
> To wait the word to fire?

It was called *First Drums Heard* and there were three more verses. When the war brought moments of explicit fear I find, looking back, that I reacted in three ways. One was to pray, another was to fall asleep and the third was to become rather ostentatiously brave or foolhardy. For instance, airborne on D-Day 1944 over the invasion area, I had a few moments of deep sleep. During street fighting in Paris, I showed off in a foolhardy manner. Aboard the cruiser *HMS Eurylus* in the Mediterranean, I shut myself in a round house and prayed when she began to fire her guns. These were specific and relatively brief episodes. I was never tested by prolonged fear of the kind which produces heroes of conscience. I am not proud of my reactions, least of all the praying, though I am still given to performing them.

It is too easy to blame others or circumstances for finding oneself in a spiritual desert. It is also too easy to omit this subject altogether in writing about one's life. Easiest of all is to leave it till some crisis blows the mind and you are on your knees on the comfortless stones of that desert beneath an empty sky.

The expletive praying to God is almost a superstition, a pitiful attempt at one-shot magic. It is only a little more articulate than crossing your fingers going beneath a ladder, avoiding the sight of the tail of a piebald horse, turning money at a new moon, or, if you are bi-lingual as my second wife Moggie is, calling out loudly three times at the sight of a single magpie, "Pie! *Je te salue!*" I dare not speak for others on a subject like this, but I suspect there are many like me to whom prayer becomes an expletive habit and lingers on from one crisis to another.

I became conscious of this in the early fifties, when I went through a longish grey period of depression which did not show. Everything went rattling on, work, leisure, family life, I tried my usual slogan in times of adversity—"John, write your way out of it". But by this time I was drained of poetry and was to enter into a ten year period of drought. I tried to think my way out of it. For the first time I experienced the shakes. It also occurred to me that alcohol was not necessarily a comforter, and that sweet oblivion was bought sleep as unrequiting as bought love. In the full flood of life there was no-one I could talk to about the grey cloud over me. My close friends were drinking companions and people who came into my professional daily life. My wife Crystal was the mother of my children who, I thought, should not be burdened by the ugly grey of my depression. We had lost some of the intimacy of communication, a war casualty. This was my fault not hers.

I was alone with only myself to blame for my isolation, not in solitude but in the midst of life. And, of course, I looked round to see who and what I could blame. God came first. Other people seemed to have God to fall back on, why not I? My mother had been close to God in an easy, relaxed, though conventional way. Yet, after I had flung a fistful of rosebuds down into her open grave, I realised that she had taken her Almighty Father with her. Before I went back to boarding-school, I took a cheap little wooden crucifix of hers, anointed it from her scent bottle, wrapped it in a scrap of purple silk, coffined it in a two-ounce tobacco tin and buried it. It was an act of finality I have never tried to rationalise.

At Gresham's we prayed a great deal—house prayers daily, chapel twice on Sunday, three times if you took communion. God hovered, clean-living, muscular, frowning at what was dirty, which included all sexual activities, threatening masturbation with blindness, smiling on those with straight bats and the administration of the Honour System—under which you went and confessed to every misdeed, unless it was something really serious. This God was regaled by a great bawling in chapel, and watched us confirmed by a retired bishop in chilly respectability. I left that one-dimensional image of God with much relief. I did not attend any church service until I went to Chiswick church to be married some nine years later. In due course we had three church christenings. These were social events complying with custom. Some years at Christmas I took the children to a carol service, they, meanwhile, having compulsory prayers at their various schools and enough religious grounding to comply with custom. We never went to church as a family or shared communion—Crystal, in fact, had never been confirmed. We lost on that. I felt an occasional twinge of regret blaming the Church of England not myself. I also had moments of envy of Roman Catholic acquaintances for their active involvement, and particularly for their celebration of Easter and Christmas. During the late forties and early fifties, Christmas Day had begun with a hangover following Christmas Eve tipples during stocking-filling and tree-decking. There was the usual over-eating and no spiritual replenishment at all.

During several months in Malta, toward the end of the Siege, I had made friends among the Jesuits and among parish priests in outlying districts. I threw away my romantic predilection for incense and ceremony and studied their Catholicism objectively. I almost convinced myself that it was logical then, travelling on into North Africa, I let it fall away.

I picked it up as a thread of hope on the heels of my blaming the established church for our spiritual destitution. Christopher Hollis, a prominent Roman Catholic writer and son of an Anglican Bishop, declared, "Blame yourself, dear John, not your church." His brassy nasal voice carried to the corners of any room he was in, though I gather it was not so effective in the House where he represented Devizes. We were lunching in one of his clubs and every other table seemed to harbour some clerical figure. When he made his pronouncement, most of these figures stiffened and there was an awful silence. I thanked him in a murmur, catching out of the corner of my eye glimpses of people discreetly looking round to see who 'dear John' might be. It was just a rough tongue. Christopher was disputatious but not fierce. He took great pains to give me an introduction to a priest at Westminster Cathedral who he thought would be 'understanding'.

Just as well, perhaps, that I do not recollect the name of that understanding priest for the mission was a failure. Once or twice a week I would go to him for instruction and coffee before rushing off to rejoin the rat-race. I began to feel that nothing was happening. I was losing my resolve and so I suspected was he. I think it was the hand of God that intervened. When I rang the bell at the appointed time, I was given a message to say that the understanding priest was in the throes of a nervous breakdown and would not be available for some time. No substitute was offered and I did not ask for one. I accepted it as an act of God.

I had become too preoccupied with denominations. Christopher Hollis was right. I gave in to a sense of failure and of course to self-pity. Why should these other people involve themselves when I was shut out? No longer portly but fat, I took on resentments like calories while maintaining an urban exterior. For the coronation of Queen Elizabeth II, I attended Westminster Abbey twice. The first time was the dress rehearsal, where I was allocated a Duchess's seat to witness the whole thing close-up minus Regina. I wrote the commentary for one of the colour films of the event, and also an eye-witness account for an agency. For the actual performance, I was in the top gallery, fitted with chutes for sending copy to Fleet Street and with portable loos. Here, I shared my flask of brandy with a clergyman connected with the choir who had belted out *Vivat Regina*. Here too, amid all the splendour and pageantry, I learned the reality of the establishment of the Church of England—that the Queen was enthroned as the head of it. Difficult to imagine Edward VII or George IV filling this role ...

From 1954, the break-up of my family life began and Crystal and I were divorced in the following year. It would have been so much more bearable if I had dried out and faced the calamity with a clear head and some spiritual stamina, but by this time I had isolated myself more and more not only from friends and affections, but from realities. For a time I let myself drown in grief for the loss of family life which I had always yearned for since the death of my mother. For the break-up, we moved into London to a Nash villa in Camden Town, with the York and Albany the nearest pub . I installed lodgers and did cooked breakfasts for some of them. I acted in what people liked to call a 'civilised way', by beaming goodwill in public and making smooth practical arrangements, while hitting out in all directions behind closed blinds. The rights and wrongs of it all are now irrelevant. But where was cake?

The thought that life was worth living emerged as cake fleetingly, to be hastily suppressed or processed to speed the production line. A suffering man of the world could not be expected to face his immature child-like nature. "When you came into the Club you would pass the time of day but you weren't really there; it used to puzzle me a lot," an old friend recalled some years later, after I had dried out.

Bitter hatred takes considerable resources to maintain, and I found it not just unrewarding but exhausting. Self-pity assisted by the bottle can run on for years. Divorce is not just an incident but a long-term perennial, influencing even grandchildren.

After the low season, Easter Week that year was generous and sunny. I had taken it into my head to go to communion the week before, to a little chilly shabby church, and I came away with wide-eyed enthusiasm for the James I liturgical text. The very sound of it was healing. I had never valued it before because I had carelessly lumped it in with the whole stock-in-trade of the Established Church. That Easter was not just a four day break with the smart turn-outs hoofing it in Regent's Park, it was a celebration. There was cake and I ate it. Monteverdi, Bach, Mozart came flooding into my life all to the glory of God—who ceased to be an Old Man in the Sky or a deity shut in some church or an icon kept in the corner of a room. No matter what the externals, God was a presence inside my nature, a mystery.

After Easter, I celebrated my betrothal to Monica Grant Forbes—instantly christened Moggie by my family and friends, to the consternation of hers. We were married as soon as the divorce was made absolute.

The blessing of the Church of England, of which we were both communicants, was hard to come by. We were both 'innocent parties' in dissolved marriages. As such, we had been welcome at Holy Communion with our respective children, some of whom had, at that time, just been confirmed. By marrying with the support of the children on both sides, we were barred from the sacrament—until we had been looked over by a clergyman. This outlandish ecclesiastical procedure was courteously explained on the telephone when I stated that our case was urgent. We wanted to take the children on the first Sunday of the holidays that they would spend with Moggie and myself, as man and wife. "We have to see what sort of people you are," said the voice on the telephone, "we have to consult the Bishop."

This seemed so curious that I sought advice outside the parish. Because of his reputation as a liberal-minded man, I consulted Canon John Collins of St Paul's. Could we take our first communion with him? He could see for himself what manner of people we were. He was having lunch with us at that time. But he hedged; in such matters at least he was a rigorist. Clearly our presence would embarrass him. APH was at that time writing *Made for Man*, a novel closely concerned with such problems. His advice was awesome: he wanted us to sue the bishop, no less, on the grounds that refusal to take us as communicants was a slight upon our characters.

Having had quite enough of the law, I decided that this kind of test case, even if it had the full support of my former father-in-law, offered a depressing opening gambit for a new marriage. We therefore meekly submitted ourselves for ecclesiastical inspection. What window dressing was desirable? The gin bottle might perhaps be hidden, together with my copy of *Villon*, bawdily illustrated by Dubout, presented to me by the artist in Paris on the day of the Liberation. Actresses and other manifestations of high life would have to be barred from the doors during the visitation. How else could one prove respectability in the eyes of the Church?

The visit was arranged at an unequivocal late afternoon hour, at which it could not be supposed that we would attempt to bribe the Church with tea or with liquor. My wife arrayed herself with due modesty and kept asking whether the Church would want to look all over the house. I put on my formal clothes I keep for meetings of the Obscene Libel Committee, and reassured her with promises that I would keep the clergyman pinned down to an upright chair by the fire and strictly to the ecclesiastical business in hand.

The clergyman came a little early. And what a large glossy resplendent pillar of the Church had stepped out of the pages of Trollope to look us over! Nor had I had any need to feel any qualms about actresses, for our visitor was the Rev. John Baddeley, brother of Hermione and Angela. Our conversation ranged over the theatre, literature and London life. My wife played the piano, sang some little French songs and demonstrated a garlic squeezer in the kitchen. He left with the promise that he would speak to the Bishop that very evening and that all would be well. It was all very pleasant, but quite fantastical, this method by which the Church granted us its sanction to accompany our children to early service the following Sunday.

Re-marriage brought family life to the home. We moved back to the country, to Ashdown Forest, and I had a *pied-à-terre* in London. In spite of happiness and domestic contentment, resentment stayed on. Adaptation to stepchildren was a problem. I began to avoid problems. I told myself I was the only individual who had to undergo such domestic stress. I was heading for over-drink. To summarise, I thinned down and dried out, saw love everywhere and before, not after, these events and was writing poetry again after a lapse of ten years or so. It was published, but I see now that it was juvenilia.

It would be ridiculously immodest and smug to claim any special relationship with God. Yet a rediscovery of faith, very private and unassuming, not in any way a conversion to a denomination, is of such significance that it would be dishonest to ignore it or gloss over it. It demands no props. It is there in the Mass, in the James I English or Series III, be it said in a great church, at my hospital bedside or in my study.

THANK GOODNESS FOR CAKE

It is there in music, in the love of people, in the wet pavements, in compassion given and received, in sharing and communication. I tried to celebrate it in this poem—*Praying*:

>Hear the thunder
>Under the pavement
>Growling to get out
>And rain
>Seething to find air.
>Feel
>A tight
>Hood of summer clamped
>Down over damp hair,
>The dreams
>That hoped in pockets
>And planned escapes
>Pinioned by screams
>With soundproof edges.
>
>Such are palpable threats,
>Recognised with the gloss of daylight
>On waking furniture,
>No bigger than a lip bruise
>Upon the acts of love.
>
>How to find prayers
>Not just for amelioration,
>Not for the crops,
>For money,
>For right-handed children,
>For relief from
>The landlords of the mind
>Those loudspeakers,
>Saying there is no God.
>
>Prayers to get past.

Prayers to go without shame,
Tremble proudly out,
Sometimes speaking a language of tears
Or laughing
With the sweetness of the humble
The strength of the condemned
With nothing left to lose.

Prayers too proud to be seen.
Too fierce to stop at altars.
They are the insignia,
They get past
In the bright disguise of silence
When the public praying
Has been turned on to full blast.

They can find the ear of God
Between two bodies,
Or in the liturgy of birth,
Or the sacrament of dying,
Also in the aching solitudes of
Ordinary hours
Stretched to ordinary days and nights.

It occurred to me that cake could be an identification with God. But I dismissed the thought as being too facile. It would seem like waiting for divine inspiration, whereas it is a moment of truth in the human being, of precious 'immaturity', of childlike wonder. Could it not be the prayer from me to God?

Bertie Lomas the poet argues, "Why is it too facile? While God's existence can't be explained, neither can the universe's, and it seems much more certain that God exists than that we do on the universe we select out of the vast unknown.

"If God exists, he must have all that we have and much more; that includes personality and an interest in personalities. Are not the moments you call cake the moments when, not we approach Him, but He approaches us? And isn't the reason Mass makes sense that He has bound himself to approach us in that?"

Yes. I think closeness to God. I dare go no further.

Going Down

In the fifties, my working life shifted into Bloomsbury and publishing, with sorties to Soho to write film documentaries. Since escaping from the property world in my twenties, I had retained a perverse hankering for business. I had had a little publishing experience as part-time adviser to Bertram Christian in the thirties. My qualifications, so long dormant, included a pass in the Law of Contract. With this slender equipment, I eagerly took an appointment as literary director, part-time, with Evans Brothers, educational publishers who were adding books of non-fiction to their list. I was able to withdraw from some of the stress of freelance journalism. The pace was leisurely and the occupation still considered gentlemanly. They were patient with me as I learned the essential facts of finance, sales and distribution. I was surprised, so were they, that I took to all this non-literary side with relish. The office boy of my youth had been promoted at last. Given that grounding, a literary director was considered a literary man whose efforts were not always to be taken too seriously in a largish organisation. In a small firm he had more chance to mix his activities. His position nevertheless remains that of a semi-amateur among professionals. Since then, publishing has been hectically dragging itself into the twentieth century. I wish I could have been the right age to have gone into the business in the late seventies, by which time the occupation-for-gentleman had really gone, though country-living aunts and mothers still take pride in any member of the family in publishing, on account of its respectability and the image of luncheons with eminent authors.

However streamlined, programmed and modernised, publishing still demands some of the intuitions of a good farmer. A sense of timing and of the intellectual climate. A flair for subjects and people. Inspired guesswork at how many to print, supported by advice from the sales people, market research being virtually impossible with each item a unique product, not a range.

One bestseller which I fathered was *The Dam Busters*. The Air Ministry gave me the squadron history. I found Paul Brickhill languishing out of work, gave him his subject and he did a great job. Then the experts wondered aloud whether there was really any demand for war books. It was hinted that because I had been in the RAF, I had allowed my enthusiasm to get just a little out of hand; so only a few thousand were printed. Sales were a quarter of a million within quite a short time. I made no faces at the experts. It might have been so terrible the other way round—with tens of thousands ordered and a few thousand sold.

Another war book I commissioned was *The White Rabbit*, the story of Wing Commander Yeo-Thomas told by Bruce Marshall. Tommy had suffered permanent injuries at the hands of the Gestapo and managed to live through a concentration camp. In Paris in the fifties, he was back in the couturier business with Molyneux, an unlikely setting for such a man of action. He had already ceased to hate the Germans, even members of the Gestapo. He was confident that the hordes from the east would carry communism to the English Channel. To mark his concern for my safety, he told me in the fragrant salon in the Rue de la Paix that he would send something to my London office to protect me. Weeks later, a man in a greasy mac dumped a dirty brown paper parcel addressed to J. Pudney with the receptionist, and left without a word. It contained a well-oiled revolver with a small but useful quantity of ammunition.

Later, after I had joined Putnams and we ran along on a shoestring with a takeover the ultimate fate, the month of August would find me the only director aboard. I enjoyed this, dabbling with affairs normally outside my territory. One sunny morning, I had just signed the cheques with a long-faced accountant (it wasn't a good month), when the management of the Royal Festival Hall came through. Would I at once confirm the booking? "Sorry," I said, "I haven't ordered any seats."

"No, no. The booking is for the Royal Festival Hall itself." The voice went on to give the date and name the price.

We could not on that sunny morning afford to book a village hall. I played for time, said the other directors were away, and, implying that this was run-of-the-mill stuff, could he kindly give the name of the individual who initiated the order.

"Gerard Hoffnung, on behalf of his publishers Putnams. He said you would guarantee everything."

I said I would ring back within the hour. I managed to contact Hoffnung, that lovable, infuriating imp-angel. He brushed aside my worries. His high-pitched squeaky voice carried lofty assurance. "We can fill that hall twice over. Don't give it another thought." Hoffnung was a Quaker who never lied or exaggerated except with his pen or in a public performance. I took his word for it, confirmed the booking and, in due course, saw people being turned away on the night, the first of the Hoffnung concerts. That unforgettable night when Hoffnung, armed with his conductor's baton, fought a duet with his first violin; and when four brass bands burst into the auditorium, trampling the hysterical customers. Hoffnung said afterwards that the great thing about the concert was that it would sell more of his books.

I never cared greatly for the company of authors. I prefer engineers. I soon learnt that many authors show a disagreeable side of themselves to their publisher, crying aloud for instant attention, demanding impossible advertising budgets, outraged because the book is unobtainable at Luton, jibing at the jacket, etc. I therefore found myself uneasy, even downright bored in dealing with other men's books. It is the one snag in being an author-publisher.

It was of course a gregarious life, on the literary cocktail fringe, and rich with expense account lunches. In the documentary film sector, it was unusual to have any meeting with clients unless it was over lunch—and the office had its own cocktail bar. I had a diabetic scare and was put on to the 'diet of portions' by Kings College Hospital. It was not designed as a slimmer's diet but I lost weight. Nobody said not to drink so much, though it was the beginning of the well-known pattern through steady into heavy drinking and then down the slope into alcoholism.

I enjoyed scripting the films, publishing the books and the expense account luxuries, but inside there was unease and mistrust which had to be drowned. I loved my wife, who kept clear of the London scene. I did not confide in her. She had her own two children from her first marriage, a family unit within our family pattern into which I should not trespass overmuch. She had looked after her children alone for six years. Theirs was an intimacy from which I was naturally excluded. I did not want to inflict my own nebulous misgivings upon her.

This was in fact a symptom of self-isolation, and it also fed my perennial resentment at the partial loss of my own children. Against my moods of sarcasm or self-pity, my offspring and stepchildren ran up their own defences—happily long since demolished. There were other losses—love, friendship, poetry, all of them blurred. There was plenty of work. The flask began to accompany the papers in the brief case. In the country, it had a hidden corner in the wood shed.

My poetic dearth continued, and in 1957 I staged that funeral of my talent, such as it was, by publishing *Collected Poems*. It had an air of finality about it—certainly for me. For some time I had hated people who said 'written any poetry lately?' Its publication caused scarcely a ripple of critical interest. I had gone out of fashion. In the eyes of some, I was indeed defunct. When I unwisely—and no writer should ever do it—asked for my book in a large provincial bookshop, the young attendant shrugged and said, "He's dead I think. Haven't heard of him since the war."

Perhaps it was this that spurred me perversely to put pen to paper and produce a sheaf of poems. There was nothing remarkable about them, no better or worse than their predecessors in the volume. They soon earned a sheaf of rejection slips.

I then created Edward Blinco, lifting the name from a gravestone in Langley churchyard. Each poem was re-typed over his signature, provided with an accommodation address, and sent back to its source of rejection. With the first acceptance and a few guineas, I opened a bank account for Blinco. The manager, who was the only one to share the secret, said, "You've got to be thick-skinned for this, haven't you? I can't believe its good for you in the long run."

I took pleasure in Blinco's small triumphs. Entirely on acceptance of rejected Pudney work, he built up £30 in the bank. He received editorial notes such as 'Let us see more of your work.' A publisher wrote wondering if Mr Blinco was already committed or would he care to discuss book possibilities—over lunch. Finally somebody wanted one of the poems for an anthology. It was ridiculous, yet I let every triumph hurt me. Such were the vagaries of fashion!

"That may be, but you're not doing yourself any good," said the bank manager, persuading me to close the account, for the sheaf was finished with and there were no more forthcoming. I wound up the funeral proceedings by writing the story of my life as mentioned on the first page of this narrative. Looking back, I am amazed how I kept to myself and the bank manager, the Edward Blinco business and all that went with it. I had reached the beginning of a period in which I shrank from anything but casual, superficial relationships. People of my own age seemed to be boringly middle-aged but in some way better off, in achievement and contentment. The young I vaguely envied, but felt they would resent any effort I might make to get through. I was increasingly indulging in the measuring-up game. This, again, is an aspect of isolation. Everyone who comes within the range of friendship or acquaintance is assessed. "He has done so much better than me. He can't want to spend time with me ... She has become so involved, so literary, I'm sure she now despises a writer like me ... Then look at Fred, always talking sex, getting at me, there's nothing to him." You don't look for warmth, humanity, love or the need of help in these people; you measure as you talk politely or politely dodge. This, I have since discovered, was not a singularity of my own. Depressives, addicts and incipient or mature alcoholics, whom I have tried to help in some way, admit to the measuring-up game and express astonishment, or even resentment, that I should know about it—a symptom of isolation.

I have described my first and my last drink. Without over-burdening this narrative with liquor, and also without pride or self-justification, I will put down briefly what over-drink and its crisis was like, for people often ask me—after saying dreamily or condescendingly, 'I don't know how you manage without it'—a remark which would be judged uncouth if they were wondering how a diabetic manages without sugar.

Alcoholism, a dreary subject, was remote from me. It was something hidden away that happened to other people outside the familiar compass of convivial tippling. The sickness began when I took to tippling alone, and carrying about my own secret supplies of the stuff so that it should be always at hand. The convivial tippling went on with decorum, and even a show of moderation 'Carries his drink well,' etc. The lone drinking increased. I became accomplished in concealment. I judge that the pattern became an illness when the body made demands irrespective of what the head might say, or of what the social, domestic or work situation might be. The actual pleasure in the liquor itself begins to fade. Its effect on the body, comfort, solace, reassurance are what counts. Physical tension, the shakes, drying out of the mouth, inability to eat, all symptoms which a swig of spirits will ameliorate—if not for long, long enough to get by with the social, domestic or work situation in hand. Thus, a miniature cognac in the dressing gown pocket, to down just before shaving and see one through breakfast with a steady hand and reasonable appetite. Between 11.00 am and midday, working on a film commentary, a feeling of anxiety develops. It is overcome by an abrupt visit to the loo for a swig, followed by a peppermint chew. A token glass of beer with the others at lunchtime, but not feeling 'safe' to sit down and eat. Surprise! "You used to be a great one for the pub lunch." Visit an out of the way pub to nibble and drink. The work goes well enough.

Crisis time is about 4.30 pm. This can be the worst crisis in twenty-four hours. I have since discovered that it is common not only to drinkers, but to others under stress. A hospital consultant told me that this was the time when he habitually took purple hearts. After another visit to the loo for a stiffener, all is well until the convivial social drinking which follows the day's work, at which one is cautiously temperate. The evenings vary so much in activity and intake that no fair example is possible. There are always drinks on the way home or on the way to any social event. The worst evenings are alone on a solitary pub crawl, dodging acquaintances, briefly picking up strangers. After heavy sleep with bad dreams, the body becomes desperate in the small hours and a wonderfully reassuring furtive libation follows. After a time, a short time if you are lucky, this over-drink hurts. The body, apparently going through each day so normally, is secretly ill. The sooner rock bottom is hit the better.

I have perhaps over-stressed the physical nature of over-drink because it receives too little attention. The change in temperament is more readily apparent and has many unpleasant faces, truculent, morose, furtive, aggressive, cynical, suspicious, for instance. All hurt and gave hurt. The mental processes, the psychology of this illness, are fully explored during treatment, no two sufferers being alike. There is rarely just one cause, but the common denominator is isolation. The head knows what is wrong and the body cries out in pain before the sufferer acknowledges the score—sometimes exposed for him by a driving offence.

During this bad time, plunging toward rock bottom, my despair seemed to purge me occasionally. There were moments of cake at dawn or at high noon, asserting a will to live or, more modestly, something worth living for. Moments when my child-self looked at my predicament in anguish and wonder and refused to believe that it could all end like that. Such self-revelation did not carry with it the power to halt the plunge, or even to mitigate for more than a short break the despair. But amazingly, out of it came an ending of the poetry drought. No one writes poetry in their cups, but between whiles I was at it again. I make no claim as to its quality but at least it formed the foundation, like a kind of juvenilia, for the body of my work, which filled several volumes in the sixties and the seventies. Through this poetic reawakening, I found myself drawn toward the young; the generation in their teens and twenties to whom I got through in poetry readings. The days of Blinco were indeed over. These people were articulate, argumentative, irreverent. To my surprise, I established instant communication, while keeping my illness to myself.

Though these rays of light did not stop my decline, they gave me back enough of a will to live to cut through the self-pity and shout at myself to find a way of breaking out. Superficially, life was going on as usual, and I was working. I am told that the over-drink had begun to show a little, but nobody remarked on it at the time. My own family was worried about my drinking, but the idea of alcoholism took some time to grasp and, by that time, I was hysterically seeking help.

Whether actively resisted or voluntarily pursued, treatment can be fairly elusive. To begin with, alcoholism, then, was not universally recognised, even in medical circles. Some GPs share the indulgent incredulity of contemporary society. They are just too nice to take you seriously.

An old family friend, a doctor and magistrate in the north of England, said, "You're just a hard drinker, old boy. You may have your ups and downs but that's your pattern and I shouldn't worry overmuch."

A dietetic expert, a doctor with whom I had been working

on a literary project, said reassuringly that a bottle of Chambertin was equivalent, metabolically, to three potatoes. "When you talk about being an alcoholic, you're just obsessed with your physical intake."

I went to a GP under the National Health Service. Sympathetically he gave me some intensive jabs of Vitamin B. "These will put you on your feet, and it's up to you to stay there." I asked him what he did about alcoholics on a longer term basis. "Nothing much I can do about them, unless they're raving and have to be put inside. Don't get many. Don't look for them either. Their own fault usually." He shrugged, but he was not an unkindly man. "Not like you. You're just over-working. Might even get that way myself."

In these and other medical consultations, there was never a cross word. Only their inability to force me to regain control of a situation which I had already recognised to be out of hand. I could not cope alone. Some may have done so, but I knew I needed help. In the end, I got it by going into a telephone-box and ringing the National Council on Alcoholism. Their pamphlets led me directly to the writings of Dr Lincoln Williams, and to private treatment.

Being not only willing, but almost hysterically eager, I dropped everything and took a crash treatment. It lasted three weeks and it was costly; but it was suggested that I might compare the cost with my personal drink expenditure for a few months—and I took the point.

Suppose I had not had the cash, backed as it happened by private insurance. I could not have done it in the same time under the National Health. I should have had to be exceptionally lucky, or perhaps much more desperately ill to have done it at all. Though the Ministers of the Crown may recognise alcoholism as a condition of illness, too few GPs are equipped or sufficiently well-informed to cope with it. The subject does not even appear in the syllabus of some teaching hospitals. A National Health Service patient who achieves treatment is likely to receive it in the alcoholic unit of a mental health hospital. It may be thorough, but it is usually very prolonged. What, then, about his job? Being self-employed, I had all the worries, but only myself to whom to make the excuses. Most people have a corporate or individual boss whose views on alcoholism may be progressive, reactionary or just rule of thumb. Safe for the employee to take time out for heart trouble, TB, asthma, a broken limb, even VD (What? At your age?), but risks attend those seeking sick leave for alcoholism. "We can't employ drunks. We have our image to consider."

I had no employer to square and, with this advantage, I decided to 'go public' as an alcoholic, contributing what I could toward bringing the subject out from under the stone and mitigating the social stigma. Warning notes sounded but I went on a Frost programme on television, using my own name, and wrote a piece in the *Sunday Times Magazine* which must have affected many, for people produced cuttings for years afterwards. The exposure did no harm but was not to be carried to the point of becoming a drink-bore, the Alcoholic Poet ... The stigma existed, but was negligible in potency. Work was not affected. Before the crisis, Courage, the brewers, had been talking over the possibility of my writing a book about the Group. Its management history included Mrs Thrale, whose sale of the business evoked Dr Johnson's immortal line of sales talk: "We are not here to sell a parcel of boilers and vats, but the potentiality of growing rich, beyond the dreams of avarice." It was a good commercial subject, mostly set on the London tideway, which attracted me. I imagined them reading about me as an alcoholic, and had just written off the project when they came through with an invitation to do the book. My public declarations did not worry them. So I spent the first year of my recovery in and out of breweries, a fairly exacting therapy.

But, as I was discharged by Dr Lincoln Williams with awful warnings about relapses, my thoughts were no longer hunched up inside, measuring myself and others. They were displaced by loving gratitude for Moggie, who had borne the brunt of my temperamental breakdown, and a new attitude of love toward the family and friends who had supported me. I was almost dangerously light-headed. While I wrote about beer, poetry flowed.

We went to live in Greenwich. My flirtations with this place went on for about a quarter of a century. When I lived in the country, first in Kent then in Sussex, I regularly found excuses (education of the young or edification of overseas visitors) to stand on that majestic little hill beside Wren's Observatory, and look down upon Britain's most elegant palace, the Queen's House, and up-river to the unique angle-shot of St Paul's framed by Tower Bridge.

I swear I didn't start living in the place just for the view. In fact, we were not house-hunting when we side-slipped into Greenwich. We just saw an ad in the Sunday papers and, with quiet precipitation, came to live in part of the property once owned by the parents of James Wolfe. He left it, a major-general at the age of 32, and returned, embalmed from the triumph of Quebec in 1759, to lie in state for some days on the ground floor. One of his letters described it as being 'the prettiest situated house in England'. I was a bit carried away myself, discovering that I could see St Paul's from the back loo and Westminster's Victoria Tower (flag and all sometimes) from a window we reinstated in my study. Views are bad for writers; and when the chestnut candles came out that spring I became convinced I should never set pen to paper again.

That was soon overcome by the realisation that Greenwich is a working place. Rich in vistas and history may be, but enjoying a uniquely varied and brisk contemporary life. It is a commuters' suburb where, nevertheless, foreign seamen frequent some of the bars. There is active industry—things are still made in the borough—yet it is a venue for international tourists. It has a live theatre, an open market, an increasing number of restaurants and an ever-increasing battery of juggernaut traffic. A lot goes on. It's a good all the year round place to live in with no danger of becoming a bourgeois ghetto—and I have not had to brick up my study window again to exclude the view.

Coming Up

Approaching the near distance and the present, a narrative such as this becomes increasingly difficult to write with proper honesty. One lacks objectivity. One is too close to living people to write of them with the frankness they deserve. This is particularly true of cherished friends who are under thirty and in a first flowering. In addition to such inhibitions, (a reason why less rash autobiographers confine themselves to their childhood and early youth where most of the characters are out of the way), it is easier to recall calamity and to celebrate good times. I came into better times, it seemed, through acquiring a new humility, not self-esteem but self-knowledge. Even to declare that much implies a certain lack of modesty. Coming out of alcoholism (we call it recovery not cure), I was full of love; but not saintly or holy, just glad to be alive and over eager to make up for lost time, to make amends. A change in temperament takes place almost overnight. Second childhood is a familiar symptom of old age, but this was more a manifestation of second youth rather tiresomely imposing itself at the age of fifty-five. It was brash, uncomfortable and a potential nuisance to my family. For me, so long as I could control it, it was fun.

I published three volumes of new poetry in the course of five years, and then a paperback, *Selected Poems 1967-1973*, reprinting the better ones with more new work. The doctors suggested that the recovery treatment had re-started me as a poet. I challenged this: "Nearly half the poems in the first book were written while I was still on the bottle. The rest, since recovery. If you can tell which is which, I'll be in grateful awe of you as doctors. I don't remember myself."

The new poems drew me closer to the young. I was invited to universities not by the management, but by the students. Readings were quite unlike the ladylike affairs of the thirties. At Sheffield, I was put on at midnight, with a second stint at 1.30 am. At Lancaster, also in the middle of the night, a mixed but well-paired audience lay on the floor holding hands, from time to time making critical noises and applauding. The oddest recital I gave was at a smallish pop festival in Sussex, where they said, "Around the cooking fire about midnight would be nice."

My first two poems mentioned death.

"We don't want fucking Death. Give us Love!" came from the audience.

I did one called *Aspect of Love*.

"Do it again and again ..."

I did it. The words of much pop music are singularly repetitive so poetry was expected to be like that. I did several love poems a number of times. They were appreciative. Then I noticed ripples of movement round the fire. Were they bored and preparing to wander off into the night?

They were, in fact, resolutely and decorously taking off their clothes.

"Do I strip too?" I asked the girl who was holding a light for me to read by.

"I can't stand here holding your trousers, mate, can I? Keep 'em on, I should. Nobody will mind."

It had begun to drizzle. I was glad to keep them on. I concluded with a couple of fun poems and was presented with a dish of macrobiotic food. A policeman—in plain clothes, or fancy dress, rather, because his attire was semi-hippy in order to be unobtrusive—asked me my age. When I said I was just into my sixties, he said, "You ought to know better."

"I was just functioning as a poet," I said heedlessly.

"Don't come across poets," he said, "but I should have thought they were steadier than that."

The police were involved in my most profitable poetry reading. After a performance at York Festival, I was driving down the motorway early in the morning with the sunshine-roof open. I was wearing my pink denim suit and I was singing. I had not noticed how the speedometer had crept over 100 mph until lights flashed and the police car headed me into the side.

"Get out, please. How old are you?" said No.1—obsessed as they all seem to be with age.

"A thousand years old," I joked, and fell flat.

"Where have you been?"

"At York Festival, reading poetry."

"Poetry!" exclaimed No.2, as if I had said I had been swallowing goldfish.

"Yes, poetry," I cried desperately. "Have some now." I reached for my book and gave them *Aspect of Love*, an impassioned rendering against the whoosh of traffic.

They both smiled and No.1 said, "Makes a change, that does."

I was winning. "I've got another one with a motorway in it. It's called *Morning*."

I reached round but couldn't find it among the papers on the back seat and apologised.

"Your licence is out of date," said No.2.

"There now," I quavered. "Must have forgotten that too."

They whispered ominously together. Then No.2 brightened up.

"I suppose poets have their heads in the clouds. Just report to your local police station with your licence and insurance, will you." They wished me good morning and departed without a word said about speed. *Aspect of Love* had saved a £50 fine and a much dreaded endorsement.

As I approached the age of sixty, I grew out of that euphoric second youth; but I kept my affectionate relationships with the younger people, half a generation younger than my own children. I did not go out of my way to seek them out. Ignoring the yawning age gap, I found I was talking the same language, stimulated by sometimes abrasive argument, enjoying for the first time in my life outspoken 'workshop' criticism of every poem I wrote, and handing it out. No talk of tendencies and influences, just is this hard or soft, and 'that's a lousy line' or 'that's great'. Gavin Henderson, who in his twenties was running the Philharmonia Orchestra and also the York Festival, taught me more about music, while still in his teens, than I had acquired in the course of a quarter of a century.

A most valuable lesson was his assertion that there are no harps in Haydn. This has stood me in good stead for years now—and I recommend it as a conversational weapon—of defence. When you find yourself really threatened by musical bore talk—not musicians' shop, which can be delightful, but by the know-all heavies who take a score along to a performance—you have only to lead the conversation toward, harps or toward Haydn. Then casually, but loud and clear, you declare, "Of course there are no harps in Haydn." This dries them up instantly and gives you the status of real authority. What you do with it is your own affair.

Nobody of his age was talking about the war, income tax or

the good old days. The focus was on the present and the immediate future. There was compassion and tolerance, which I often found lacking in my own generation. Their acceptance of alcoholism, for instance, was casual, concerned yet uncritical. On a pub crawl some drunk would drink a skinful, but nobody would say my non-alcoholic tipples were spoiling the show. So unlike a scene in Fleet Street, where an old acquaintance and colleague literally twisted my arm so that it hurt for days afterwards, brandishing a double malt whisky. "All this nonsense about going teetotal. I'm not. I'm not letting you go till you take this for old times sake, even if I have to pour it over you."

At Brighton, after a poetry reading, I stood a last round before closing time, and ordered a rather turgid and fattening Pepsi Cola for myself. A certain Andy, at that time about twenty and going into the technical side of films, had had a skinful of Worthington. He suddenly put down his glass and glared at me with suspicion. "What have you got in that drink of yours?"

I told him, but he snatched up my glass and sniffed it. "I'm not so sure. You haven't put something into it? You're not falling by the wayside?"

I was protesting that I was not having any relapse, when Andy interrupted. "We're taking no chances..." He gulped the whole of my drink down.

Five minutes later, I had to hold his head while he was sick. A Pepsi on top of all those Worthingtons. It was heroic. I put it on record as one of the greatest acts of friendship, though at the time we roundly abused one another.

On a January night in 1967, Moggie was driving us home to our Ashdown Forest cottage from a dinner party. There was snow in the air and already a thin coating on the ground. Crossing an exposed stretch of the Forest, we were caught by violent gusts of snow-filled wind. Momentarily blinded and out of control, we pitched off the road and ended upside down in a drift among gorse bushes.

By stripping off top coats, we managed to squeeze through a window. We knew where we were exactly. It was the most isolated section of a side road. The nearest telephone would be three or four miles off. It was snowing fitfully as we groped our way back toward the road. I was just thinking what a lucky break, when I saw the lights of a car heading the way we had been going. I staggered into the road, in time, as I thought, to flag it down.

The car hit me, tossed me over the roof, and I landed on my left shoulder. I was conscious of it all, the crunch as my legs were hit and broken, the curiously soft thump of landing on my deltoid. I saw the back of the car as it slowed up. Then I was stricken to see it accelerate and vanish into the night.

I crawled to the roadside bank and Moggie, herself with a badly bruised knee, set off to raise the alarm. I was alone until a party of young people returning from a night out in Brighton spotted the lights of the overturned car and found me. Lightheadedly, I sang them extracts from *The Beggar's Opera* because they seemed to think I was going to die. While I was alone, with the cold gnawing into my body and snow lightly dusting me over, I felt a chilly presence of death which I could only hold off, I thought, by staying awake. Fortunately, I was no longer fat and was in good condition. I had swum a couple of lengths at the Olympic Pool at Crystal Palace only the evening before. I then found myself speaking comfortable words to my loved ones; then to my friends. What a contrast to the nights when I lay alone and isolated with over-drink. The very warmth of love, the feeling anyway that they would go on living; these thoughts held off that chilly presence nudging my numbing body. This recital of people was like an impromptu prayer. It kept me alive for an hour and a half till the ambulance came. Somebody said, "He's been talking to himself and singing. It's shock."

After weeks in King's College Hospital, my legs attached to two weighted pulleys, myself able only to sit up and lie down, no turning, they told me that I would have to learn to walk. The initiation was a trip by wheelchair to the hydrotherapy room. It was a circular pool, raised so that the warm water came up to the average person's armpits. After all the weeks of inaction, it was a novelty to be undressed by the buxom nurse who had brought me and squeezed into swimming trunks. "Wait a minute I have to get ready for this," she said, signalling the assistants to lift me into the chair, like a ducking stool, in which I was to be winched up and swung round to drop into the pool. Apprehensively, I went up and was gently manoeuvred over the steaming water. "Don't let me drown. Remember I'm helpless," I implored them. "Not to worry, I'll catch you." My nurse reappeared, entering the pool clad in a bikini. I descended into her arms. Apart from the delicious surprise (I had often thought of cuddling her), her support was vital. Even in water, I could not stand on my feet, and I realized for the first time that walking was an accomplishment which would have to be learnt. Instead, we just waltzed in the water.

There were people with far worse injuries than mine coming to the pool, many of them motor-cyclists. A boy they called Steve floated like a lily, with his arms and legs at grotesque angles and a smile on his young serene face, while a nurse worked on his spastic-like hands in the water. He was a sports car casualty. The classical beauty of his features contrasting with the hideous disorder of his limbs haunted me for a long time. I heard later that they restored his speech and faculties, and mended his body. Only ten years ago they told me such therapy hardly existed, and Steve would have lingered on as a cabbage.

Some time after, I was on my feet again and I wrote a three act play called *Ted*, based on Steve. It was networked as a television play and had a short run afterwards on the stage at Leatherhead. I was gratified by the number of people who wept on the first night. I hesitate to inflict my story line, but it turned out to be a parable.

Ted is re-built, physically and mentally. As he recovers, he rejects his father, his girl-friend, and finally the doctor who has directed the therapy. They all expect him to be the same young Ted. They unconsciously begin to reject him when they find a new personality, A temperamental stranger. They try to re-adjust but fail, or reluctantly take on a new role.

I had no thought of my own life when I wrote it. More recently, after the play had been acted on stage it occurred to me that Ted, though he was based on my observations of Steve, had some relevance to myself, not so much in terms of people as in values. I had not gone back searching to restore the values and the qualities in life which had drowned during the post-war years and middle age. I had ceased to look for my mother in every woman. I had ceased to play the measuring game. It meant looking at people as if discovering them for the first time. If they were boring, cynical, lascivious or aggressive I wasn't to dodge or dismiss them, but make a positive contact—admittedly this led to some sudden retreats. Then I attempted to discriminate, to work for quality rather than quantity. For half a lifetime, nobody of my own generation had needled me toward this. Now it was Nigel Hamilton, more than three decades my junior with very sharp needles indeed, saying aloud what I had hardly dared to say to myself, and certainly not what my contemporaries would have concerned themselves to say.

He helped to select and arrange my *Selected Poems*, of which *Take This Orange* was one. He pushed me from time to time toward autobiography. Here is one of his pushes.

"At best I see it as I saw *Take This Orange*: a gift, fashioned with skill and love, for now; but able to call on a lifetime of other selves, other lives, other people, other moments. My own biographical ear holds a jumble of memories, things you've said at different times, bits floating from your work. To put them together, in all humility, not as an example to the world or anything pontifical, but merely as, at last, your own rendering of what happened, from the start to this strange moment now, having made your way through death to see summer in Greenwich and films of yourself in shorts by the Sphinx."

It was not all take. I found I was giving out to people. I was sharing in the lives of more people, and more people were sharing in mine—a fact that came home when I was lying helpless with my broken legs and which fortified me for what was to come. I recognise now that I was sometimes ruthless, demanding, reckless on days when the air smelt of autumn bonfires.

Reverting to the Ted parable. Where had all the social and political idealism gone? Belonging to the Labour Party was no longer a cause but a habit, a defensive measure because the alternatives were distasteful. I like the rich when they keep a good table, are in some way creative with their wealth and not obsessed with social and political power. The poor, the underprivileged, the have-nots? I identify with such social outrage as homelessness, but for me the hard line definitions of right and left are blurred. We built the Welfare State that we wanted— or some of it. What dismays me is the managerial bureaucracy which envelopes it. We were always stressing the need for *planning* from the platforms of the forties and fifties. I, for one, never thought who the planners were likely to be. I still don't know. There was much talk about imaginative projects but what emerged have too often been designs for mediocrity or unimaginative blunders, such as high-rise flats. The political obsession with education, the aim of which was levelling, should have been a levelling-up, not down. Nobody seems to notice it too much—I still get and accept invitations to a box at Ascot and a box at Covent Garden—a major revolution has in fact taken place. The workers through the Trade Unions, and the shop stewards are ruling the country. Something very near the dictatorship of the proletariat has arrived. With much idealism killed off, as Ted killed off his bourgeois background and his slightly shifty conventional dad, I favour seeking what is good and supporting it, though it may not be a conventional political issue—conservation rather than conservatism.

I have been much in and out of squats. I found among the younger society that inhabits those fringes of urban life, an apolitical outlook, a sometimes coarse knocking of conventional values, a good-natured contempt for the media—they are never telly-orientated—and an acceptance from birth that society will provide their keep. The apparent fecklessness does not entirely conceal certain compassionate moral values.

From a squat in Camberwell where Julian Branston lives, who at the age of twenty has already published a volume of poetry, comes this:

> The world belongs to one who stole
> his politics from a playing child
> using geography not to calculate
> altitudes but for the love of boundaries ...

And his encouraging advice about writing this narrative was worth having.

> Please be very critical with yourself over what you write. You can write with compassion and wit, making everything timeless—making yourself a cool, uncluttered space through which you summon emotion and keep it dry, clear, concise—not weeping, or running, or squeezed dry. Remember you're not writing for your life. It's just a good time to write an autobiography. You have a dozen more things to write about.

I am not even disillusioned any more. I am on the look-out for what is new and good, and I try to recognise it with a loud cry when it crops up. I do not expect myself to become older and wiser. I do not believe all progress to be beneficial. I favour materialism, even as I have seen it in the United States, but it must be used not accepted as a way of life. I like a fast car but I don't want it to have any social or moral significance. (And I'm not looking for endorsements.)

I do not press the Ted parable further. For me, it shows the need for acceptance of change in temperament and personality without hurting anyone, without needing to have an accident. It should take its own time.

At periods of life, not least moving from middle-age into ageing, such temperamental changes are frequent and should be acknowledged. In the more lush years of my middle-age, I refused to acknowledge them myself. Too late, many parents find they are losing touch with their offspring; they rigidly adhere to their image as grown-ups who—to use the sickening jargon—'know better'. Their young in return rigidly treat them as parents rather than friends or ordinary human beings, thus reinforcing the generation gap. The adulation of the young which became a cult in the early seventies is silly and, incidentally, like Christmas, sustained by commercial exploitation. Automatic veneration of the old, respect for experience, I regard with suspicion. A necessary part of the structure in the past and in tribal societies, but a divisive influence in our own. People are people. They do not require labelling 'young' or 'old'.

During the years following the hit-and-run accident, I shook off my rather mixed up second youth and settled into my sixties. How much I prefer these times to the twenties and early thirties when my first youth was rampaging. Those times were haunted by mounting fears in which my generation was always being told that it would be so much worse than the last lot, which we had as children escaped. The fear in the seventies has become identified with life, and lived with for a long time. It is not something you point to in a corner of the room. For the younger generation, it is taken for granted, like television or jet flight. People are more articulate and better informed. Few people seemed to know where Czechoslovakia was in the 1938 crisis. Even Ministers described it as a long way off.

Television is blamed for many evils in society in the seventies. So far from enslaving me I watch it standing up and, according to my family, 'fidgeting'. Yet its overall effect is clearly good. People know where places are, become accustomed to witness events as they happen, and listen to well-informed argument. This more than makes up for the unacceptable violence and sex. By comparison, the twenties were dark indeed.

There was little music in my life then; just *how* little is reflected in *Guide No.3* published by the London Underground (Railway, not drop-out organisation), in 1924, at one shilling:

> Concert Halls—Chief among these are the Albert Hall and Queen's Hall. Special concerts are given at the former from time to time, including Sundays, at which the leading singers and musicians appear; and during the

Winter season there are Promenade Concerts and Ballad Concerts, among other features. Queen's Hall is notable for Promenade Concerts (August-October), and for special concerts by the London Symphony Orchestra, the Royal Philharmonic Society, and the New Queen's Hall Orchestra. Here again, and with respect to the Crystal Palace concerts, the Central and the Kingsway halls, and to the smaller halls (Wigmore, Aeolian, etc) where recitals are given, the newspapers should be consulted. During the Winter months Sunday concerts are given at the Music Halls.

No mention of ballet. 'Covent Garden is, of course, notable for Grand Opera.' A little music came through the early radio sets. There were no long-playing records and relatively few gramophones. What a desert compared with the concert pages of Sunday newspapers in the seventies. Whether the quality was better or worse is not for me to judge, but the availability and diversity of the arts has improved out of all knowledge. No young person can possibly feel culturally deprived in the seventies.

Nil By Mouth

Ten years almost to the day after the accident, I became aware of a catch in my throat. X-rays showed a shadow. An oesophogoscopy confirmed that there was a malignant growth in my throat—cancer. I was in rude health, within a few days of my sixty-fifth birthday. I had been enjoying dancing and winter swimming and hard work in my Greenwich garden. Moggie was with me at every consultation; she was there when the surgeon, a lovely woman with arresting blue eyes, broke the news. We went about in a state of shock until our family doctor came and sat with us. He talked with frankness and lucidity about options. I found it best to accept this news as if it were that sudden accident in the snow—irreversible, to be lived with. When my legs were smashed, I handed over my body to those who were to treat it and, with them, looked at myself from outside. I was not indifferent. I was co-operative and usually obedient. With the rest of myself I went on living to the full, as far as circumstances would allow. I have six grandchildren. The older ones read my fun poems aloud, snatching the book from hand to hand. They have not been cajoled or coaxed to do this, so the spontaneity is flattering. How individual they are already. In spite of family likeness, each affirms a whole character, the beginnings of a personality which will mature after I have gone. My love for Moggie and my, by this time, grown up family was intensified, and at the same time I fell lightly in love with some of the nurses.

This was to happen again over cancer. Unconditional surrender to the fact. The body to be passive, detached, the mind and spirit to be alert and positive. This I have tried to achieve ever since that January day when I was marked down.

I went to Guy's Hospital and was only in bed for a few days. Radium treatment was decided on and Guy's are particularly well-equipped for that. The hospital is only about three miles from my Greenwich home, so I took the course of treatment as an out-patient. The day I went in, I had a contract from the BBC to write and appear in a film about Thomas Cook the excursionist, about whom I had once written a book. The BBC was prepared to take the risk of my not being able to carry this through. It involved filming in the Midlands, in Switzerland (Thomas Cook 'invented' Switzerland) and in Egypt. At least I could write the script, an activity which went well with the radiation treatment, and from which I suffered few side effects. Meanwhile, we used the word cancer and made no polite evasions. There were waves of sympathy, some from most unlikely directions, creating a sense of goodwill which was rewarding. Not least were the unadorned comments of the young, such as, "You will try and live the year out, won't you?"

There was a pause after the radiation. Then the verdict 'there is now no trace of malignancy'. An instinct told me not to celebrate. I still had to have my oesophagus dilated from time to time. Clearly it was damaged and I had choking fits, though I managed to continue with the filming. For years I had been preaching that one should seek diversity and change of work as one grew older. This was practising that precept with a vengeance. I had to learn all the lines—no prompter—and talk into the eye of the camera in all manner of public places such as London Airport, Granby Street Leicester or the footbridge at Geneva. Nothing like it had ever happened before. The camera crew, who knew where to bang me on the back when I choked, turned an alarming experience into a most stimulating exploit.

Back from Egypt, I went into Guy's for what were becoming routine dilatations. Afterwards I was told that the cancer had returned. I was grateful for the instinct which had held back the celebrating. In the pause before the next treatment, I hastened to the BBC and recorded the whole of my off-camera commentary.

Then things went wrong with the oesophagus and it had to be replaced by a tube. Only great skills saved me at Guy's. For several days Moggie came and slept in the hospital. My mind and spirit were detached from my body. In a moment of cake I looked at myself with wonder and my voice said, "John, you may be dying." I turned to Moggie and those near and dear and prayed for their lives. For myself I was numb, looking at myself.

Just before Christmas, the worst was over and I was transferred to Greenwich Hospital for the beginning of cytotoxic treatment, a programme of twenty injections spread over ten weeks, with an array of side effects threatened. My hair might drop out, for instance. So a wig-maker suddenly appeared, taking measurements and copying my hair-style. They must have thought the calamity would be sudden for the wig was delivered within a few days. Quite a lot came out on the comb during the ensuing weeks, but I was in fact spared the indignity of sudden baldness.

Worse was to come. A tracheotomy—a silver pipe put into the throat. They do it to racehorses. This relieved breathing trouble but deprived me of my speaking voice. I was left with a whisper. Home again after this and formidable readjustments. It is virtually impossible to initiate telephone calls unless the person the other end knows one's predicament and does not keep on saying "Speak up, caller". No more public poetry readings or speaking one's work aloud, a necessary part of composition. People either whisper back or shout. One can't call the dog. I had begun to write this narrative; it became therapeutic. The BBC lacked three sentences from me to complete the film. For a week or so we waited in case my voice came back. Then they had to find somebody to act me. This was done so well that I couldn't spot the three sentences when the film was shown.

I find you cannot do much with a whisper. Getting angry verbally, for instance; you just have to throw things. The first time I threw a book at my wife she very properly shouted back, then turned the other cheek by saying, "You must be feeling better today."

Radiation had weakened tissues and a fistula developed, causing food to leak into my windpipe. I was beginning to starve. I had long since got my figure back. Now I was running fast the other way. The answer to this was gastrostomy.

Harassed by food rationing during the First World War, my mother used to say, "If only we could give up eating and just have pills or take it through a tube."

Her wish was fulfilled for me at least forty-four years after her death, when I looked down through an anaesthetic hangover and made the acquaintance of a tube and spigot protruding from the left side of my stomach wall. The hospital warning note NIL BY MOUTH over the bed was familiar. It proclaimed a temporary fast essential for an operation or a barium X-ray. This time it was there for good. I had had a gastrostomy so all food and drink had direct access to my stomach. Writing these lines soon afterwards, I marvel how really portentous events take so little time. The divorce proceedings which ended my first marriage after twenty years took fourteen minutes. They told me the gastrostomy, ending sixty-eight years of eating by mouth, took about the same time.

Having the stuff pumped in, following the prolonged and frightening struggles to eat and drink conventionally, was such a relief at first that the implications were hidden in clouds of euphoria.

The reality of my loss began with yearnings for a boiled egg. I think it is the first food I remember. The performance of opening it, learning to tap the thinner end, being allowed to 'take the top off'. The horror if it were either hard or too runny. Special treats, the speckled eggs, laid by my favourite Plymouth Rock. The precision, the individuality, the completeness, of a boiled egg! The unique taste which nevertheless varied interestingly from one boiled egg to another throughout a lifetime. (Let us forget, momentarily, the man-inflicted graduations of farm-fresh, factory-produced, free-range, shop-stale eggs.) Guinea-fowl eggs, duck's eggs (my father preferred them with cold pickled pork), bantams', plovers', gulls' eggs hard-boiled. Yet it is the soft boiling of a hen's egg 'just right' which can bring marriages to the brink or speed a mistress on her way.

At times during the war, any egg became a rare luxury. The most glamorous for me was the goose egg, admittedly *sur le plat*, served as a main course at Claridges. I was a guest so I do not know what this golden egg cost. In Malta, toward the end of the siege, we were offered pigeon-size hen's eggs at three shillings each. But the reality of a boiled egg never hit me so hard as when I watched them pumping the stuff into me beneath the NIL BY MOUTH notice, and listened to a comforting voice, "This will do you good. It contains three eggs." So that was how eggs were to be! Not another boiled egg in my life! And a right good cue for self-pity, this.

So back to that bleak subject—deprivation. To be deprived from one moment to the next of the pleasures of eating. 'You can put things in your mouth, have a chew and put them out. You may even swallow the taste of the thing ..."

It was a case of working on deprivation all over again, keeping self-pity out. No established or organised therapy exists. Grateful for the life-saving gastrostomy the patient must come to terms with the personal, domestic and social implications and from the first day with the question *What does it really feel like?*

I was fortunate, at least, in having some rehearsal, the experience of giving up drink and then tobacco—the first a deprivation imposed by the threat of a moral and physical breakdown, the second a self-imposition with health and aesthetic pressures. The food by mouth deprivation was a sudden drastic medical necessity, and here the continuing experience of the other two helped. Had I anything of the saint or the holy man in me, or of the philosophy which Teilhard de Chardin evokes as 'the forces of diminishment', if these deprivations were spiritual or were touched with nobility, they would be more edifying. Nevertheless, they are not to be thought of as punishment. One has not been singled out by some Calvinistic predestination. There are too many people in the world starving, too many in prison, too many deprived of too much or under duress for one to be stricken by any sense of singularity. So when the Devil began his blandishments with, "look at the way everyone else is enjoying this summer with juicy smoked-salmon followed by strawberries and cream", it was no good trying to block out the dainties and to forget them. Far better to relish them in the mind, celebrate the times and places when they gave most pleasure and be grateful that they still exist for others. It was a temptation to lie awake desolately pondering favourite items—pork crackling, new fresh homemade bread, pheasant well-hung, treacle-tart, asparagus from the garden—and all the carefree privileged people consuming them. Far better, though, to lull oneself to sleep thinking not only how enjoyable these were, but that the so-called privileged ones still tucking in were no wiser or godlier, and were just as likely to lie awake worrying as I was.

This, for many of us, has been a first-line recovery from over-drink. The alcoholic who must give it up, which he must for ever, must realise his parity with his fellows. Those fastidious friends round the polished table at the club, the merry young people at the pub round the corner, old George lifting his pint after digging the garden, are not privileged. They are no richer or poorer in spirit, in sociability, in love, in work because they happen to drink. There is nothing wrong in them, enjoying what I enjoyed for so many years. I am not diminished. I can join everyone of them in friendship and drink something of my choice that isn't alcoholic. I do not shun company. I stand my round. I keep and serve liquor in the home.

This parity which, fully realised, gets rid of the deprivation bogey, is not a mere defensive or passive attitude. Some genial aggression may well reinforce it. "Do you tolerate me simply because I drink?" has been addressed to those who begin to make heavy weather of abstinence. To the man who spots one with a soft drink and says, "Are you still drinking *that* stuff?" I recommend a steady, (smiling) glance at the Scotch in his fist and, "Are *you* still drinking *that* stuff?"

"It's whisky, best malt whisky, what's wrong with that?" It is an affront to point at his Scotch, yet derisive questions about soft drinks are fair game. Keep a little compassion, though.

The fellow is probably worried about his own drinking.

About food, there is no need to be aggressive unless people start boring you with diets. You can kill that scene with a shrug, "I just don't eat anything." Those who force culinary advice and boast of their exploits in the kitchen, can be quickly overcome, I have found, with a recital of a typical day's menu which my wife Moggie administered to me through the tube. (For my mouth, a token sip of each meal to keep up with the taste that tum is getting.) This for instance:

BREAKFAST	LUNCHEON	TEA	DINNER
banana	watercress and onion	dried apricot pulp	avocado
goat's yoghurt			tomato
lemon juice and honey	cream cheese and egg	yoghurt and honey	sesame cream soya milk
Caloreen	Casilan (protein)	Caloreen	Casilan

I go back to alcohol, and especially to smoking, for the next point which is one of priorities. While not turning one's back on the pleasures of the kitchen and the table, one must not become obsessed with them. Let the thought of it all settle into the background. Let its significance diminish.

Drink absolutely dictates the life patterns of the alcoholic. How to obtain supplies and how to dispose of empties (you daren't use your own dustbin, and the antics of the unacknowledged alcoholic with his empties is the surest giveaway to his condition). Every hour of every day is tempered by the availability of the stuff and furtive means of using it. Not only the metabolism, but the social structure of life are ruled by this tyrannical priority.

Treatment and the first stages of recovery cause it to slip from the top of the list. It is gradually edged out because so many things, not least human relationships, are more important. For years I have kept a broached bottle of Scotch in my workroom (behind the Trollopes on the bookshelves, where it used to be hidden for quick regular tippling). Its presence there spells out the message that I am not deprived, the availability is there, but the priority has vanished. This is not a smug touch, rather it is an item of personal industrial archaeology.

Overt companions of the atrophied Scotch are the tobacco jar and a cherished Dunhill pipe, with their message 'we're still here if you want us again'. An open pack of French cigarettes beside them is for current hospitality. This might appear sentimental and smug. Yet it was, and is, an important aid to the therapy of giving up tobacco. Addictive smoking asserts a priority as tyrannous and more subtle than that of drink. Neither society nor the individual demand secrecy about it. Indeed, the addict is often boastful about it. That first one of the day! The joy of it when the rested and awakened palate takes its initial assault! The rituals of giving and taking which are built into the social structure. But with it, the anxiety to stock. Never, in spite of the slot-machines, to run out. The miles I travelled across country for an ounce of tobacco. The deviations in London to take in the only café— in Fleet Street—where the stuff was available all night. From sixteen to sixty years of age I was happy in this bondage, gratifyingly masculine, deft in operation, soothing company in the solitudes of writing. Why give it up?

I had no threat of cancer when I did it, no special worries about the health hazard. I simply wondered why I had to cart a bit of wood about in my mouth, with occasional tubes to replace it in polite society. How ugly, messy and time-consuming it all was. Looking not only at myself, but at even the most beautiful creatures smoking, what a blemish! Why spend so much time, energy, and money on a pleasure which half the time was distasteful, ultimately downright harmful, and aesthetically uncouth.

The way to give up is to attack the priority by stealth, indifference and good-humoured neglect. It should be a non-event and should provide fun. Do not begin on New Year's Day, your birthday or even a Monday. Surprise yourself mid-morning or mid-afternoon, not even looking at the clock, by putting down a half-finished smoke, cigarette, pipe or aromatic cigar, saying, "That's the last ever." Don't tell anyone. Don't cut off supplies but, after buying in a few day's stock, continue to pay yourself—childish money-box pleasure this. Forget when you started. Observe how family and friends continue not to notice the change. When they do, play it very casually. You won't remember when and you don't really know why you gave it up. In any case, you are keeping stocks and paraphernalia in case you should want to take it up again. You offer the pack round. You have not set up as anti-smoking, or as a health freak. By this time, the priority has toppled; and a keen sense of liberation can blow through the smoke and across the sordid ashtrays like a summer-scented breeze.

I do not remember even the year when I put the Dunhill on the shelf, and that disposal of a priority is the kind of exercise that can help the first stresses of giving up eating. The social problems are formidable compared with those of non-drink and non-smoke. Intimate friends and children may enjoy the rituals of tube-feeding, and even participate. For the rest, eating out means taking your own food and equipment. A 'meal' only takes a few minutes. Afterwards, one can join the company at table and accept token titbits, like a grown-up baby and, if well-conditioned in anti-deprivation, this is not an unpleasant way of spending the time.

When I started writing this narrative, I could still eat cake.

NIL BY MOUTH

As I finished, cake has ceased to be a reality for me, though spiritually and symbolically it is more potent than ever. I now say Thank God for Cake. For those I shall leave behind, I offer:

> The price I pay for my dying
> Is its cost to others
> Who, to rid themselves of me,
> Suffer.
> Pray now that I may leave them
> Enough
> To sustain their loss.

Afterword

Some men grow old gracefully; others find life increasingly tiresome as they age. John Pudney belonged to neither category. Instead he seemed to find in advancing years his second youth: a passionate rediscovery of life's excitement. He resigned from his London club; gave up alcohol; refused to attend cocktail parties or indeed any socialite gathering; even gave up his beloved pipe. The poetry that had ceased to flow after the last war suddenly burst forth.

To say he lived to write would be to misunderstand the nature of John's transformation. A series of events—early success, marriage to the daughter of A. P. Herbert, and fame during the Second World War as an RAF poet—led him towards a gruelling middle-age. Divorce, alcoholism, demoralisation were reflected in extravagant journalism and a dearth of creativity. "I wrote for money and for drink," he once explained to me. Reviewers began to disregard his books as the work of a hack. Besides, it was an opportunity to settle old scores, to pay out his early celebrity.

And then, in his late fifties, the muse returned reflecting a new positivism in his life. He had married again, an adoring, devoted companion who restored his belief in himself. The next decision was to seek help in overcoming alcoholism. He emerged a new man and never touched a a drop of alcohol again. The story of John's last years is

AFTERWORD

one of moral regeneration: of finding faith in himself, in others, and in God.

A near-mortal accident in the snow on Ashdown Forest merely increased his determination to live again (an episode mirrored in his stage and TV play *Ted*). His marriage to Monica gave him courage; his friendship with men and women became an almost mystical confirmation of life's purpose.

It was at this time that I first met John, as a customer in my bookshop at Greenwich. He had recently moved to a flat in James Wolfe's old house on the edge of Greenwich Royal Park, with magnificent views of London and the Thames. This new home was to add to the inspiration that now characterised his life.

The Thames began to figure prolifically in both his poetry and prose. He celebrated the bridges and tunnels crossing the tideway in *Crossing London's River* and wrote a musical play on the life of Brunel which, in turn, led him to write on London's rapidly dying docks.

He was not distressed that his books failed to excite great critical interest. He loved writing as he loved life and the opportunity to write on subjects that inspired him rather than on hack commissions was its own reward.

His poetry grew steadily more authoritative, culminating in his volume *Take This Orange* which celebrated the meeting of two generations. If BBC radio found his verse insufficiently intellectual to take up, poetry societies and universities clamoured for him to read from his new work. He had a unique delivery, throwing his lines from deep in his throat with a slight nasal damping.

In time he began to promote his own readings in Greenwich together with young poets on board the *Cutty Sark* which became a yearly and crowded event.

And then, when his creativity seemed to be reaching a pinnacle and his home had become a sort of literary workshop, a cultural centre in south-east London, he found he had cancer of the throat.

The story of how John faced up to this diagnosis, and the way he refused to allow the disease or its treatment to interrupt his literary output is one that no one who witnessed it can ever forget; as was the dedication of his wife Monica by whose efforts John was able to challenge what seemed like inevitable death at Christmas 1976 and survive a further year.

I mention this because, without her efforts, this very book could not have been written. John had written to me in the summer of '76 when I was living in Finland, enclosing the first chapter of this book. With its strange, effortless movement between past and present—part recitatif, part analytical—I found it as exciting as his major poems. As he sent me chapter after chapter for my objective criticism, I could only marvel at the way this dear friend, in his sixty-ninth year and suffering from terminal cancer, unable to speak except through a metal tube, unable to eat except through a tube inserted through his stomach, had put together such a brilliant evocation of his childhood and career. This 'anti-autobiography' as he called it, thinking of his official 1970 version, *Home And Away*.

At his funeral, Father Paul Jobson extolled John's greatest virtue: his unashamed, uninhibited capacity for love. This quality was reflected in all his later works but perhaps most of all in this, John's joyful, celebratory account, tongue-in-cheek, self-mocking and yet tender, of a far from perfect but ultimately unregretted and profoundly happy life.

Nigel Hamilton